TOM PRYCE

MEMORIES OF A WELSH F1 STAR BY THOSE WHO KNEW HIM

(Eric Lemuet Collection)

DEDICATION

To my Granddaughter, Niamh. The way you deal with not just your disability, but with the multitude of issues that come your way, and still achieve international success when representing your country, inspires me on a daily basis and helps me see life in a completely different way.
Darren Banks

To Amelia and Daniel. I hope, in years to come, you will read this book and find in Thomas Maldwyn Pryce an inspirational role model.
Kevin Guthrie

First published November 2020
Copyright Darren Banks and Kevin Guthrie

Authors Darren Banks and Kevin Guthrie
Editor David Tremayne
Designer Sarah Scrimshaw

Front cover Eder Costa Barcellos
Rear cover Peter McFadyen

Printed by The Manson Group, United Kingdom

ISBN 978-0-9576450-7-3   **Publisher** Performance Publishing Ltd

CONTRIBUTORS

TONY TRIMMER	22	TIM COGMAN	65	ENID TOFT	118
ANDY ROSS	24	IAN PHILLIPS	66	ANDREW MARRIOTT	126
PETER WILLIAMS	25	ADRIAN L JONES / ALWYN WILLIAMS	69	CLAIRE JONES	128
MIKE DOODSON	26	RICK MORRIS	70	RAY ALLEN	129
ALAN CORNOCK	28	JOHN GENTRY / ROGER SILMAN	71	ANDREW HARRIS	130
TED WENTZ	30	CHRIS MARSHALL	72	NEIL TRUNDLE	132
DAVE RICHARDS	32	DAVID J ROBERTS	75	JEAN-PIERRE JARIER	136
JOHN WATSON	34	KARL JONES	76	ELWYN VAUGHAN	137
MIKE WILDS	36	ALAN REES	84	MIKE HILLMAN	138
DANNY SULLIVAN	37	DAVE JONES	86	DEWI ROGERS	140
TONY SOUTHGATE	38	MARTIN WEBB	94	NEVIILLE HAY / PETE LYONS	141
TREFOR WILLIAMS	42	TONY VLASSOPOLUS	96	ANDY HALLBERY	142
RICHARD PEACOCK	44	BUZZ BUZAGLO	97	DAVID HUGHES	144
RONDEL MEMORIES	54	TREVOR FOSTER	98	BILL MOFFAT/ ROD MCCULLY	145
TIM SCHENKEN	55	DEBBIE JONES	102	BRIAN JONES	146
CLIVE WALTON	55	ALUN JONES	104	CLEDWYN ASHFORD	148
PRESTON ANDERSON	56	IAN FLUX	106	DAVID WILLIAMS	149
JONATHAN GREAVES	57	EDDIE KNIPE	108	JOHN HANKIN	150
PAUL GOY	58	JACKIE OLIVER	110	TOBY ST. GEORGE MATTHEWS	152
GORONWY 'GRON' STOREY JONES	59	JORGE KOECHLIN	112	JAMES BECKETT	154
DAVE LUCKETT	60	NICK JORDAN	115	CHRIS JACKSON	157
BARRY BOOR	64	BOB HEWITT	116	NELLA PRYCE	158

A NOTE FROM THE AUTHORS

All contributions were obtained between September 2019 and March 2020, and have all been approved and checked by each individual. While there is some inevitable repetition we feel that each person had their own individual memories of Thomas Maldwyn Pryce, so therefore we felt they should be left as they were.

In the recollections of the people who knew Tom from his early days in North Wales they knew him only as Maldwyn or Mald – Tom or Thomas came when he moved to Brands Hatch in 1970 – so therefore, we have used Maldwyn/ Mald throughout their contributions.

ACKNOWLEDGEMENTS

When we embarked on this project, just over a year ago, we had realistic expectations of what we could achieve. Due to the generosity, effort and kindness of a vast number of people we feel we have exceeded all these.

To Nella Pryce, a lady of immense class and fortitude, a thank you of the highest order for agreeing to write such a moving and heartfelt foreword. We cannot begin to imagine how you would undertake such an onerous task. We can only hope we have, in some way, repaid your efforts by remembering your beloved Thomas in a way you find agreeable.

To all the contributors – over sixty of them – we offer our sincere appreciation of the time, effort and courtesy you have shown us at all times. You certainly didn't need much in the way of encouragement to talk openly and freely about a loved and much missed husband, friend, colleague and rival. A book is only as good as its words. We have been overwhelmed by the sheer quality of your offerings. It has been a humbling and emotional experience, and one we have thoroughly enjoyed at every stage. It's been a privilege and an honour to have been a part of such a worthwhile project. Thank you.

Apart from the contributors other people have played an equally important part in seeing the project through to its conclusion; Simon Arron, for help and contacts; Alan Bowles, for interviewing Brian Jones face to face and help at all times; Mike Jiggle of *Auto Tradition* magazine, for help in getting the word out and support at all times; Pauline Marron, PA to Dave Richards, for help; Iain Nicolson, for help with all things photographic; Andreas Riehl, for help with Jutta Fausel; Lorraine Scouller, for proof-reading and editing; Simon Stiel, for contacts; Judy Stropus, of the RRDC, for contacts; Ian Wagstaff, for contacts; Chris Witty, for help with Chris Marshall.

In making sure the finished book reached the quality a person of Tom's stature deserved a massive thank you to the highly acclaimed journalist and author of more books than is humanly possible, David Tremayne. It came as no surprise when David offered his services immediately on hearing of our project. He is, of course, the author of *The Lost Generation*, which is the definitive, detailed biography of not just Tom's career, but those of Roger Williamson and Tony Brise. If you wish to read more about Tom (or Roger, or Tony) we urge you to track down a copy.

On the publishing front another massive thank you to Adam Wilkins and his dedicated, talented team at Performance Publishing. Again, like David Tremayne, Adam was 100 percent supportive of the project once he got wind of it, offering the services of his designer, Sarah Scrimshaw, at a very charitable rate, and generously offering to print the book at cost to maximise profits for such a worthy cause. We look forward to working with them again on future projects.

A special mention is warranted for a quite remarkable individual by the name of Dave Jones. While our names adorn the cover this is as much Dave's book as ours. He was instrumental in getting Nella on board, worked tirelessly to track down people local to him in North Wales who may have known Tom in his early days, and was helpfulness personified at all times. An added bonus, when working on projects such as this, is the calibre of the people you come across. Dave, as a human being, is of the highest quality and has strived to keep the memory of Thomas Maldwyn Pryce alive since that fateful day over 43 years ago. If we obtain your seal of approval then we know we have done justice to the memory of someone who is never far from your thoughts. Your parting words at the conclusion of our first meeting was that we were now life-long friends. We sincerely hope that will be the case.

On a personal level Darren would like to thank: My ever-supportive wife, Ann, for being so understanding and tolerant during my absence from everyday domestic matters, and who has listened to my many mutterings and tales, without the faintest idea of who Tom Pryce was, but with an interest due to her understanding of how much projects such as this mean to me. You are one very special lady. Much love.

To my co-author and great friend, Kevin Guthrie. It's been a privilege and an honour to collaborate with someone so enthusiastic, knowledgeable and patient. I sincerely hope this is the first of many more projects to come.

Kevin would like to thank: My partner Tracy, for tolerating my obsession with the sport for so many years, and many more to come! My parents Brian and Christine, for the childhood trips to Silverstone from Scotland which fired my interest in racing. Finally, to Darren, who has become a great friend over the last few years. It has been a joy to work with someone so diligent and thorough in their research.

Poetry in motion. **(Grand Prix Photo/Peter Nygaard)**

PHOTO ACKNOWLEDGEMENTS

The following people gave us permission to use their images completely free of charge, and could not have been more accommodating and patient. Unfortunately, the limitation of space prevented the use of images from some of the names below. Nonetheless, your offer at the time was highly appreciated.

Trevor Alloway; Preston Anderson; Cledwyn Ashford; Pete Austin; James Beckett; Jeff Bloxham; Keith Booker; Giovanni Buffoni; Peter Carey; Peter Collins; Gary Critcher, of the Supercharged Collection; John M Davies; Stuart Dent; John Dunn; Jutta Fausel; Mike Flynn; Hans Fohr; John Gauerke; Kevin Guthrie; Mike Hayward; Andrew Harris; Henk Hazelaar; Richard Heseltine; Bob Hewitt; Alun Jones; Dave Jones; Udo Klinkel; Paul Kooyman; Eric Lemuet; Maureen Magee, c/o Mike Jiggle; Tim Marshall; Ed McDonough; Peter McFadyen; Geoff Mitchell; Peter Nygaard; Julian Nowell; Jim Oakman; Kenneth Olausson; Phil Parfitt; Rob Petersen; Nella Pryce; Jonathan Ranger; Andy Ross; Enid Toft; Tony Trimmer; Chris Walker/Kartpix; Mark Welch; Paul Woloschuk.

Tom with his hands full. **(James Beckett Collection)**

(Eric Lemuet Collection)

FOREWORD
NELLA PRYCE

Although it is a great honour to be asked to contribute a chapter and the foreword to this book, I did not accept without considerable thought as it is inevitable that these memories of Thomas would plunge me back into a previous life of so long ago with its tragic ending.

Co-authors and good friends, Darren Banks and Kevin Guthrie, both share a passion for the sport of the Seventies and Eighties, which clearly shows in the meticulous research and crafting of this book, so generously undertaken to raise funds for a memorial of Thomas, in Denbigh, North Wales. Darren, who first got involved in motorsport at the tender age of fifteen when his brother bought a Formula Ford 1600, has previously written an acclaimed biography of Stephen South, a rising star of that period. Kevin, whose interest began through his Grandmother with stock car racing when he was only five years old, wrote an equally acclaimed biography of fellow Scot, Jim Crawford.

This book is a delightful compilation of personal memories and photographs from a wide variety of people who either knew Thomas in his youth, his adult life, his early school days or, in some cases, throughout his life. Others met him during his motor racing career, while others never actually met him, but admired his flamboyant driving style and achievements in the sport and became fans.

One thing is clear, he was universally liked and held in high regard. Aside from motor racing memories, there are anecdotes with funny and touching stories from people who knew him well, that give a new insight into the man behind the five black stripes.

Many of his current fans are too young to have seen him race, yet despite this he still captures their imagination. Perhaps this is due to his humble beginnings from a loving family, who so generously encouraged his natural talent and determination. That he is still remembered with such affection, not only in his native Wales but worldwide, more than forty years after his death is a testament to the man he was.

I think he's almost become a sort of James Dean of motor racing; he was handsome, incredibly talented and destined for great success; a special being cut down in his prime.

To me, he will always be that fun, caring, handsome young man with a terrific sense of humour and that great smile; the man I fell in love with and married, who also just happened to become a world-famous Grand Prix driver.

It is with much appreciation that I thank Darren and Kevin for producing such a moving account of Thomas's life, with so many cherished memories. My hope is that this book will keep his memory alive, and in doing so, continue to inspire and encourage others to reach for, and achieve, their own personal goals.

Nella Pryce
South of France
May 2020

Nella, pictured a couple of years ago with her dog, Bobby. (Nella Pryce).

One of Nella's favourite photos of Thomas and herself. **(Unknown)**

DAVID TREMAYNE

Motorsport Writer and Author of The Lost Generation

Thomas Maldwyn Pryce. There has not been a month, probably not even a week, that has gone by in the intervening years since that fateful day of March 5th, 1977, when he has been far from my thoughts. Sounds like hyperbole, doesn't it? But it's true. My life evolved from the industrial shelving I was building after gaining my Economics degree, into the motorsport writing career that I began that October, which has since taken me around the world many times in the course of reporting on almost 570 grands prix and scribbling more than 50 books.

Tom, and the other members of that lost generation, Roger Williamson and Tony Brise, were always along for the rollercoaster ride. (Their photos were even among others I carried in the STAY GOLD jetcar when we hit 297mph and then got upside down at 260. I thought they might enjoy the run.) They continued to live in my heart long after fate took them, fallen brothers whose memories it has long been a mission to preserve.

But what was it about Tom that first attracted my attention? How could anyone you never met become that special, that you would not only never forget them, but carry them in that most secret of places?

I guess that initially I liked what I read about him being shy. It made me feel comfortable, because I was at the stage in my life where I felt the same, before I gained a measure of self-confidence and became the sometimes loud and opinionated lifer that some people in F1 press rooms across the globe perceive me to be. It was why I revered Jim Clark, because though he was so clearly the greatest – for me, the best of the best – he fundamentally remained the same humble man that he had been when he set out on his journey.

In this beautiful book, there is a memory from Goronwy 'Gron' Storey Jones about bumping into Tom outside a pub, after Tom had become a famous F1 driver, and how he just talked to Gron as if they were still young men about to embark on their adult lives. It so reminded me of the tale J. McNeil Brown told. He was a friend of Jim's from their local rallying days in 1956, and was at a US GP one year when a hand clapped him on the shoulder and a voice said, "Neil, what the hell are you doing here?" In all the intensity of a grand prix weekend, Jim had greeted him all those years later like it was yesterday.

People who don't get up themselves, who don't become insular and aloof with the onset of fame – they're the ones I really respect, especially when they happen to be race drivers. People who stay true to themselves.

I saw many similarities between Tom and Jimmy. There was that social reserve, that quietness when they were out of the cockpit, that preference for solitude rather than the limelight, that self-effacing manner. And the way that each would bite his nails, which was more a habit than anything to do with pre-match nerves, for both were preternaturally calm. And slow to anger. And the way that the act of getting into the cockpit of a race car somehow completed them, placed them in the element for which they had been born and endowed with fantastic natural talent. It didn't matter that they drove with very different styles, Jimmy's silky smooth, Tom's much more like the sideways brio of Jimmy's friend and rival Jochen Rindt, or Ronnie Peterson and Gilles Villeneuve.

Their skill and characters drew me. Their reserve, yet also their quiet inner knowledge of their greatness which called for no outward confirmation from them. And their loyalty, often the rarest commodity in the frenetic realm of racing; Jimmy's to Colin Chapman and Lotus, Tom's to Alan Rees and Shadow. Loyalty, integrity, honesty. Big things that have always been at the top of my personal list. Things by which I judge the character of others, not least race drivers.

I still remember the time I had gone as a fan to the 1972 *Daily Express* International Trophy race at Silverstone and how, when I was walking through the support paddock that was located on the Club Straight at that big meeting, I saw Tom standing by the black Royale RP11 that he would drive. Tom Pryce! I was beginning to follow him the way I did eventual F3 race winner Roger Williamson, and Tony Brise. And there was he, standing on his own. I knew nothing then about him being taciturn and monosyllabic with people he didn't know, but that would have been academic. I was much more concerned with my own shyness. Eventually I plucked up the courage to go and speak with him, but I was too late. Just then a mechanic came out of the DJ Bond truck and engaged him in conversation, and my moment was gone. I never

Tom, tucked in behind another member of The Lost Generation, Roger Williamson, at a Zandvoort Formula Three race in 1972. **(Rob Petersen)**

did get to speak to the man who would have so much influence in my life that later, when our first son was born, Trish and I called him Tom, after Thomas Maldwyn Pryce. Any parent will understand that burden of naming, the importance of choosing something that will serve that precious little person well in their life.

Photographer Bob Hewitt speaks in this book of how much hope there was within Tom's legion of fans. And he is absolutely right. When you hitch yourself to someone's star as a fan, the hope is what drives everything along. You hope that they will be safe and will do well. Each race they do is an excitement in itself. Another step towards the big goal. It's great when you feel the momentum building. I remember following practice in newspapers back in the Seventies, long before

the internet had even been thought of, back in the days before every moment of every race was televised. You'd look for your driver's name in the list of practice times. Feel a buzz the higher up they were. Days later you'd read about his race.

Hope. That was what propelled it all. And that was what hurt so much every time there was a fallen brother day. That feeling that life would move on without them ever having the chance to fulfil the potential you saw in them. In all three cases with the Lost Generation boys, the random cruelty of their passing was what turned all that hope into such awful despair. The knowledge that they would no longer have their chance to shine, that others would take their place. Like quicksand swallowing another victim, life would move on for others leaving no trace above the surface yet

indelible scars on those who were left behind with just their memories.

Like the 68 people interviewed for this book, I remember exactly what I was doing on March 5th, 1977.

I was eight months away from achieving my ambition and starting my career in journalism, and since leaving uni I had been filling in working with a guy called Pat Boylen, building Dexion structures. Amusingly, his company was named Erection Services. That Pat. My mate Pete Finch and I were getting some overtime, slinging up some shelving in a warehouse somewhere in Maidenhead. Pete had a beaten-up Hillman Super Minx with a radio, and I would keep skidding in and out to pick up what was happening at Kyalami in the South African Grand Prix. In those days the race wasn't transmitted live, you just got updated bulletins and it was these to which I would listen avidly. The news about Tom was devastating.

Later I would research the accident in minute detail for *The Lost Generation*. And here is an apposite moment to mention by name the young man to whom others have alluded in this book without identifying him. The younger marshal who ran across the track, and whose fire extinguisher hit and killed Tom, was called Frederik 'Frikkie' Jansen van Vuuren and he worked in the ticket office at Jan Smuts Airport. As Nella's father had so empathically said to her once, his family were mourning too. I used to rail at this unknown kid, but later came to appreciate that he had simply been a young man, wanting to do his best on what must have been one of the biggest, proudest days of his life.

There were no villains that day, apart from the person who stole Tom's wedding ring. But I do wish I had been able to ask Renzo Zorzi why, when he had known for a lap that his car had a problem with its fuel metering unit, he hadn't just come into the pits instead of carrying on and then stopping where he did, just over the brow on the main straight opposite the pits. It was a secret, and perhaps a private regret, that he took to his grave in May, 2015.

For me, the aftermath of the deaths of Roger, Tony and Tom was where The Mission was born. I had always been upset, since Jimmy's death in 1968, each and every time that something horrible happened. But their incidents helped me to understand the anger I always felt, and to channel it through the pledge I made to myself never to let such heroic young men be forgotten. That was also where the seeds of *The Lost Generation* were sown, in those agonising moments of despair long before my career as a writer got off the ground. Just

as I had always known that I was going to write a book about my first hero, Donald Campbell, I knew I would write a book about them. Certainly, by the time our Tom came along in 1984 *The Lost Generation* was consolidating itself in my head, title and content. It was born not just of frustration that so many people I met in F1 had heard of none of them, or, worse, had forgotten them, but of the always simmering anger that fate could have been so callous. That they had Been Left Behind!

Nothing will ever dissuade me from the view that the 1977 Austrian GP, which Alan Jones won for Shadow, would have been Tom's first win, hands down. Imagine if he had been the man that Frank Williams and Patrick Head had chosen to drive for Williams... Ah, the pain of what might have been...

I met Ashley Judd at a Scottish Motor Racing Club dinner one year, when her husband Dario Franchitti introduced us. "Remember when I was crying in bed the other night when I was reading that book *The Lost Generation*?" he said to her. "Well, this is the guy who was responsible."

Writing that book was no trip to Paris. While finally sitting down and fleshing it out and then opening the vein was cathartic and assuaged much of the guilt I carried for not having started on it sooner, there were many times when I was glad that my computer's keyboard must have been waterproof and that I was writing in private.

I was privileged to meet Jack and Gwyneth Pryce during the course of my research and was touched by their inner fortitude, especially as they had already lost their firstborn, David. I became very fond of them, but that didn't stop the old reserve with Pryce family members from intruding when I went to the unveiling of Tom's memorial in Ruthin in 2009. I talked with Nella and David

Richards, of course, and Tony Trimmer and Richard Peacock, but didn't want to trouble Gwyn. I figured she wouldn't remember who I was, in any case. But she approached me and gently chided me for not coming over. She gave me a hug and held tight to my arm when I told her why. "Of course I remember who you are!" she reproved, like I was some silly kid. But when you walk the tightrope of intruding into other people's lives and tragedies, no matter how careful and well-intentioned you are while seeking to do the right thing by them and not to upset them in the process of trying to tell the most honest and empathic story that you can without being indelicate or overly intrusive, that sort of thing means so much. It wasn't difficult to see where Tom got his caring nature from. Jack had passed on by then, and it was the last time I saw Gwyn. That meeting remains a little memory I treasure.

One of my many proudest moments as a father came when we were racing in Formula Honda at Anglesey, back in 2001. When our Tom started racing karts, his Project One was liveried in our colours, blue and orange, and only we knew that the five vertical orange bars on the Nassau panel and the nose, stark against the blue, represented our own little tribute to Tom Pryce. Neither of us wanted to overplay it, so long as we knew what they meant. And that day at Anglesey I was so stoked when the commentator mentioned that Tom Tremayne was named after Tom Pryce, and hoped that 'big' Tom was up there somewhere, looking down and feeling happy that he was not forgotten.

The day that the finished manuscript for this book arrived from Darren Banks and Kevin Guthrie, I had awoken realising I'd had one of those dreams that feel super-real. I was walking in a paddock at a Grand Prix somewhere, and to my right Chris

Bentley of the FIA was coming in at an angle. I said something jocular and rude to him, the way we usually do, joshing as we fell in step with a group of other FIA mates. And I realised that somebody was following right behind me. I turned, and it was Alan Henry. Dear old AH. Not the fragile AH, in the months before he was finally taken from us on March 3rd, 2016, the shell of the man that had so shocked his close friend Niki Lauda when they'd seen one another for the last time in the Silverstone paddock at the British Grand Prix in 2015. But old Al, in his prime. Dapper in grey flannels and a snazzy dark grey jumper. Smiling in that naughty little schoolboy way that he had. Like he knew something that I didn't. My rational mind said this couldn't be possible, even as I turned and just hugged and hugged and hugged him and told him how much we'd missed him. That lovely man who accepted all his rude nicknames with that easy grace and tolerance that I always admired and envied.

I know a visitation dream when I have one, and it made me sad yet happy at the same time. And when the manuscript arrived that same day it made me wonder what it all really meant. Because Al adored Tom and Nella. He had had one of those special relationships with Tom that sometimes, as a writer, you are blessed to develop. They were close, and Al had driven Tom's Shadow at Silverstone in 1975 as a test for *Motoring News*, where we had first been colleagues. And Al thought the world of Nella.

I don't know... It sounds crazy, doesn't it? But I just thought there was a lovely symmetry to that little bit of happenstance. And I know Al would have loved this book, and applauded the fact that once again somebody was making sure that his old friend wasn't forgotten.

Darren and Kevin love racing, and they get it. And this is a labour of love, full of heartfelt tributes

Tom in conversation with Alan Henry. **(Motorsport Images)**

from people who revered Tom. I'm amazed how fast they put it all together, and the depth and breadth of their research, especially as it was all done pre-lockdown. Some, touchingly, apologise for getting emotional. I remember when I gave Jorge Koechlin a copy of *The Lost Generation* in Mexico one year, he told me later that he cried. But isn't all of that the truest compliment you can pay anyone in this life? Not to be afraid to show how much you cared?

I'm proud to have played a small part in this commemoration. Because what Darren and Kevin have achieved here will forever stand as a worthy tribute to a very special young Welshman who stayed true to himself, loved his family and friends, and never changed even when he made it to the top echelon of his profession. One hell of a race car driver, who was giving it everything he had when fate reached out and he was taken far too soon.

On a cold winter afternoon in March, 1975, history was made when Tom Pryce became the first Welshman to win a Formula One race. While it was not a full-blown Grand Prix, and thus didn't count towards the coveted World Championship, the Race of Champions at Brands Hatch still contained a quality representation of the talent that was on offer at that time. The whole weekend encapsulated everything that Tom stood for, not just as a racing driver, but as a human being.

The conditions for the three-day meeting were ideal for him to display his otherworldly car control, whether it be wet, damp or bone dry. It was in the wet or damp that his exuberant, flamboyant skills shone through. Traits that he didn't transmit off-track, even remotely. You couldn't have found a more extreme opposite.

He earned pole position by a second – a huge margin, taking into account the opposition – with what some purists may have thought of as an untidy and out-of-control lap, but that was never the case with Tom. For mere mortals, perhaps, but not him. It all seemed unhurried, well within his range of capabilities. Many a time a white-gloved hand would appear atop the steering wheel as he toyed with the raw power beneath his right foot, which would be working the throttle with delicate micro-adjustments. He made it look so easy and effortless, which was far from the case.

Come the race, victory was his, but it didn't come easy. A poor start in the cold but dry conditions saw him slip down the field to fifth position but he was soon on the move, putting all his accumulated racecraft to use with some clean, fair and decisive overtaking manoeuvres. All three facets were the pillars on which he built his idea of

racing. Especially, fairness. To have won or achieved any success by being underhand or devious, call it what you will, would have been utterly unworthy of a man of Tom's upbringing and principals.

To have reached the top step of a Formula One podium only five years after he took up racing is meteoric, to say the least. All the abilities he displayed that day were the fruition of all he had learned right from his introduction at the beginners' racing school back in 1970, through the junior racing categories of Formula Ford, Formula Vee and Formula F100, to the more senior and professional, Formula Atlantic, Formula Three and Formula Two. Much success was achieved immediately, which enabled him to progress so rapidly. It wasn't money facilitating his upward charge, just sheer talent, which enabled Tom to earn the essential backing of some seasoned racing people, who knew a sure thing when they saw one. While his Mum and Dad helped initially in the early days, there was certainly no silver spoon feeding him here. Far from it.

His parents were working people. His Dad, Jack, was a policeman. His Mum, Gwyneth, a nurse who later owned and ran – very much hands-on – her own nursing home. They instilled in him a need to learn a trade for his future prosperity. He chose to be an apprentice agricultural mechanic – farming and agriculture were very much a part of his North Wales upbringing, so this was no surprise. Tom had a fascination with most things mechanical, especially cars, an interest encouraged by his Dad who was a fellow car enthusiast.

It may seem to some a logical progression towards a career in car racing, but from his background and location a trip to the moon must have seemed just as attainable.

To travel the many miles to the many racing circuits situated around England was an adventure

Enjoying the spoils of victory after the Race of Champions, 1975. (Maureen Magee/Mike Jiggle)

in itself. Brands Hatch, in Kent, in particular must almost have seemed another world. It was here that he began to learn his trade. To be a part of the racing scene he moved to live across the road from Brands Hatch. To quit his job and leave his adored and proud parents at 21 years of age illustrates his guts and determination to succeed, and he disappointed neither himself nor them. That his biggest success came at the circuit he so loved, was somehow fitting.

The final outing. Kyalami, 1977. **(Grand Prix Photo/Peter Nygaard)**

Kyalami, South Africa, March, 1977: just over two years since that joyous day at Brands Hatch. Tom was now an established star in the Formula One fraternity. His star was ascendant and his future assured. All he needed now was the right team with the right car to achieve his ambition of becoming World Champion. Unfortunately, the Shadow team for whom he drove were in decline, due mainly to loss of sponsorship. Tom, typically, had shown tremendous loyalty – another important character trait – to the team that had given him his big chance. It was clear that he would need to move on at the end of the season, to further his career. But for now he was still giving them his all – another facet that was so important to him. Never give up.

He was giving his all, fighting back after a poor start that had seen him drop down almost to last position. By lap 20 he had climbed to 13th position and was closing in on 12th place runner, Hans Stuck. On the completion of lap 21 and while preparing to pass Stuck for the position, tragedy struck. His team-mate Renzo Zorzi had stopped his car opposite the pits and a small, flash fire had briefly erupted. On seeing the fire, two marshals, situated in the pit lane, began to run across the track. The track at that point came over a brow, so they would have been unable to see any oncoming cars approaching at full speed, around 175mph. The first marshal made it across with mere inches to spare. The

second, Frikkie Jansen van Vuuren, carrying a 40lb fire extinguisher, didn't.

At that precise moment Tom was running alongside Stuck, ready to overtake him, and didn't stand the remotest chance of avoiding the marshal. He struck him head-on, flinging him like a rag doll to the side of the track. The marshal's fire extinguisher struck Tom's head, killing him instantly.

The actions of a young and blameless volunteer, who was just doing the job he had been entrusted with, took from us a racing driver of immense skill. A husband. A son. And, a man loved by the many who'd had the pleasure to cross his path at some point during his 27 years on earth.

THOMAS MALDWYN PRYCE
Born: June 11, 1949, Rossett, near Wrexham.
Parents: Jack and Gwyneth.

1950
- Moves to Hightown, Wrexham, when his Dad, Jack, joins the Police Force.

1950-53
- Moves to Brymbo, Wrexham, to live in a Police house.

1953-58
- Moves to Nantglyn, Denbighshire. Attends Nantglyn County Primary School and Fron Goch County Primary School, Denbigh.

Nantglyn School circa 1954 or '55. Maldwyn is sitting in the second row, the second from the left with Trefor Williams to his right. Also, in the photo are Colin Toft, the Holland brothers, Brian and Leslie, and Elwyn Vaughan. **(Dave Jones Collection)**

1958-61
- Moves to Towyn, Abergele. Attends Towyn Primary School.

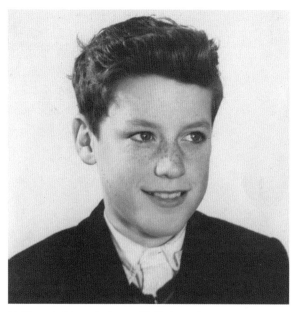

Maldwyn in his early teens. **(Nella Pryce)**

1961-63
- Moves to Rhos-on-Sea, Colwyn Bay. Attends Ysgol Emrys ap Iwan, Abergele Secondary School.

1963-69
- Moves to Denbigh. Attends Ysgol Emrys ap Iwan, Abergele Secondary School.
- Leaves school and attends Llandrillo Technical College.
- Passes his driving test and buys a Minivan.
- Begins his working life at North Wales Engineers as an apprentice agricultural mechanic.

1969
- Moves to Ruthin. Lives with his Dad. His Mum, Gwyneth, lives in Old Colwyn, where she owns a nursing home.

An early lesson in the MRS Lotus 51 FF1600, at Silverstone. **(Dave Jones Collection)**

- Attends Motor Racing Stables Racing Drivers School at Mallory Park and receives a B-plus-plus from his first instructor, Trevor Taylor, a former Formula One team-mate to the legendary Jim Clark at Team Lotus.
- Further lessons and school races at Brands Hatch and Silverstone.

1970

Jackie Stewart presents Tom with the garland, trophy and Champagne after he had clinched the Crusader Championship and with it a brand-new Lola T200 FF1600. **(Dave Jones Collection)**

- April: wins the *Daily Express* Crusader Formula Ford Championship at Silverstone. The prize: a new Lola Formula Ford 1600 worth £1500, plus free oil, fuel and tyres.

- Quits his job and moves to live at Red Webb's guesthouse near Brands Hatch to become a professional racing driver.
- June: Enters his first race at Brands Hatch, but crashes in practice after three laps and does not start.

Brands Hatch, 1971, in the Lola he had won. The five black stripes are clearly visible. These were added at the recommendation of Tom's Father, Jack, who was having trouble picking him out among a vast field of Formula Fords. (Dave Jones Collection)

- Competes in approximately 20 races, achieving five wins and a handful of lap records.
- First contact with Bob King of Royale when he asks to borrow a car to use in the newly instigated category, Formula F100.
- First appearance of his trademark five black stripes on his white helmet, at the suggestion of his Dad, who can't pick him out in a pack of Formula Fords.

1971
- Continues to race in Formula Ford with the Lola.
- Continues his association with Royale, competing in Formula F100 with TAS Racing and winning the championship with ease.

An early Formula F100 outing in a Royale RP4 at Brands Hatch, in ideal conditions for Tom. (Pete Austin)

- Races in the new Formula SuperVee category in a Royale for Toby St George Matthews in the UK and in Europe.

1972
- Signs as the Formula Three works driver for Royale.
- Scores his most important win to date by dominating the Formula Three support race at the Race of Champions, a non-championship Formula One event.
- Competes in Formula Three on even terms with the likes of Roger Williamson, Tony Brise, James Hunt and Tony Trimmer.
- Suffers a broken leg at the Monaco Formula Three race after his car broke down. While standing alongside the car attempting to fix the problem, is run into by fellow competitor Peter Lamplough.
- Returns to racing in five weeks and claims pole position at Brands Hatch.
- Victorious in the SuperVee championship after winning nearly every race he entered.

SuperVee outing, again, in a Royale at Tom's home from home, Brands Hatch. (Jeff Bloxham)

- Royale builds a Formula Atlantic car and Tom claims three consecutive pole positions in the final races of the season and wins the championship finale at Brands Hatch.

1973

Yet another outing in a Royale, this time, the RP12 Formula Atlantic car at Oulton Park. (Peter McFadyen)

- Continues to race for Royale in Formula Atlantic, winning three races and claiming numerous pole positions.
- Leaves Royale after an offer from Ron Dennis and Neil Trundle of Rondel Racing to race in Formula Two. Begins his association with Chris Meek of Titan Properties, who sponsor his efforts at Rondel.

- June: Makes his Formula Two debut at Nivelles in Belgium.
- Scores his best Formula Two result with a second place at the Norisring.

An early appearance in the Rondel Racing Motul M1, at Croft. The car was modified from Formula Two to Formula Atlantic specification for an outing at his backer/manager Chris Meek's local circuit. **(James Beckett Collection)**

- Competes in Formula Atlantic for Rondel Racing.
- Wins the prestigious Grovewood Award, given in recognition of the season's best performances by a British and Commonwealth driver.
- Meets his future wife, Fenella 'Nella' Warwick-Smith.

1974

First Formula One appearance in the Token RJ02 in the 1974 International Trophy, non-championship race at Silverstone. Despite only a brief run in practice, Tom was moving through the field before gear selection problems forced his retirement. **(Jeff Bloxham)**

- April: Makes his Formula One debut for the Token team at the non-championship Formula One International Trophy race at Silverstone. His race ends in retirement.
- May: Makes his Grand Prix debut at the Belgian Grand Prix at Nivelles in the Token. Qualifies 20th out of 32 entries. Retires in the race after running strongly in the midfield.
- Returns to Formula Three in the support race after the Token team's entry was refused for the Monaco Grand Prix, and scores an emphatic win from pole position.

First Formula One outing for the Shadow team in the 1974 Dutch Grand Prix at Zandvoort. A collision with James Hunt while approaching the first corner on the opening lap brought a very early retirement. **(Rob Petersen)**

- June: Signs to drive for the Shadow F1 team, making his first appearance at the Dutch Grand Prix.
- July: In only his third Grand Prix, qualifies an astonishing third at the French race at Dijon-Prenois.
- Earns himself 100 bottles of Champagne after being the fastest runner in the first official practice session for the British Grand Prix at Brands Hatch. Eventually qualifies in fifth place after final practice.

Tom, enjoying the free 'bubbly' he'd won. Something he did on a few occasions. **(Dave Jones Collection)**

- Signs a two-year contract with Shadow.
- Scores his first World Championship point in only his fifth Grand Prix at the next race at the daunting Nürburgring.
- Competes at the Trois-Rivières Formula Atlantic race for Fred Opert Racing.
- Runs a limited programme of Formula Two events for Chris Marshall's Baty team.

1975

- January: Rumours abound of a possible deal involving swapping places with Ronnie Peterson at Lotus, but nothing comes of them.
- March: Becomes the first Welshman to win a Formula One race when he triumphs from pole position in the non-championship Race of Champions at Brands Hatch.
- April: Marries Nella at St Bartholomew Church in Otford.

Resting on the rear wing of the Gelo Racing Mirage he shared with John Watson at the Nürburgring 1000 Kms in 1975. **(Udo Klinkel)**

- May: Makes his World Sportscar Championship debut, sharing a Georg Loos Mirage with John Watson.
- July: Becomes the only Welshman to start a Grand Prix from pole position in the British Grand Prix at Silverstone. Disappointingly, he spins out of the lead on lap 21 after encountering a rain shower.
- August: Finishes in fourth place in the German Grand Prix at the Nürburgring despite suffering from painful fuel burns to his back due to a leak. His efforts earn him the Prix Rouge et Blanc Jo Siffert award for grit and determination.
- Scores his best Grand Prix result so far and his first appearance on the podium when he finishes in third place at the Austrian Grand Prix.
- November: Makes his Formula 5000 debut at Long Beach.

In preparation for his rallying debut, Tom sampled the Lancia Stratos at the Longcross test track in Surrey for a feature in *Motoring News*. **(Richard Heseltine)**

- December: Makes his rallying debut in a Lancia Stratos on the Tour of Epynt. Unfortunately, a crash on the first stage puts him out of contention but he continues after repairs to avoid disappointing local Welsh fans who came to watch him.

1976

- January: Finishes in third place at the Brazilian Grand Prix to earn his second Grand Prix podium.
- August: Finally gets his hands on a new car, the Shadow DN8, at the Dutch Grand Prix and immediately returns to competitiveness with a fourth place finish.
- October: Finishes his year on a high with an impressive performance in the treacherous conditions at the season-ending Japanese Grand Prix. A possible victory is denied him due to an engine problem.

1977

- Stays loyal to Shadow despite other offers.
- Wednesday, 2nd March: Fastest in wet practice for the South African Grand Prix at Kyalami.
- Saturday, 5th March: While climbing back through the field after a poor start, he is killed when he strikes a marshal carrying a fire extinguisher who is crossing the track to go to the aid of the stricken car of his team-mate, Renzo Zorzi.
- Thursday, 10th March: He is laid to rest at St Bartholomew Church in Otford, Kent.

ST. BARTHOLOMEW'S CHURCH
OTFORD

THURSDAY, 10th MARCH, 1977

THOMAS M. PRYCE

1949 — 1977

(Dave Jones Collection)

TONY TRIMMER

Racing Driver and Friend

The first time I came across Tom was at the racing school at Brands Hatch. That would have been in early 1970. I was in Formula 3 and Tom was trying his luck in a Formula Ford Lola that he'd won. I remember he crashed that car quite heavily first time out, and it lay in a garage at Brands in a bad state for quite some time. I kept on at him to get it sorted. It was repairable, and I put quite a lot of effort into talking him into getting it fixed. I think I helped him repair it, and it was after that he started to shine. He did need a kick up the backside from time to time.

I watched him in one race and, as he turned into Clearways, he lost it big time. Yet somehow he held it. I mean, the car had gone. I thought there was a fair bit of skill going on there. I could appreciate exactly what was happening, and remember thinking it was almost impossible to save. I was very, very impressed. I had helped Lola develop that car in the first place, and won with it on its debut at Zandvoort. It had a lot of performance, but its short wheelbase made it a little tricky to handle.

Then Tom came to Red Webb's house. I was the first driver she had staying there. When I went to work at Brands for the racing school I walked across the road and knocked on the first door I came to. It was Red who answered, and she took me in, saying she didn't normally do that sort of thing. Goodness knows how many people passed through there by the end. She started to make it a business, and did a very good job. What a character she was! She told you exactly what she thought, whether you'd met her before or not. She was very affected by Tom's death, no doubt about that.

Tom and I shared the house for three years or so. I guess he moved out when he met Nella and they bought a house together. We had separate rooms, but it was only a small house. We had breakfast, lunch and evening meals together. Of course, I got to know him exceedingly well.

It was his car control that first focused my mind and made me think that Tom was a proper driver. If the speed is there to start with you can fine tune the rest. He was definitely over-driving to begin with. It was his skill that was getting him out of a lot of situations which he really shouldn't have been in. But that's how everybody starts, isn't it? You learn by your mistakes.

Tom could be quite hard work sometimes. He was a quiet guy and it was quite difficult to get him to come out to the pub with you. He was quite an introvert. He would sit in the front room of Red's house and not say anything for hours and hours. But, if you could get him out, he was one of the boys straight away. A bit strange to my mind, to start with. My overriding memory of that time and the time spent with Tom was definitely the fun we had. He just needed a push, and a couple of beers usually helped. His father was a policeman. I met him quite a few times. He was a really nice guy, and a bit overawed by the whole thing, as was Tom really. He couldn't see his own talent for a while. Obviously others spotted it and the thing took off.

Tom and I were virtually the same size. We were both skinny and about the same height. I could sit in his car and drive it and vice versa, without changing anything. When I had my Maki F1 outing they asked me to go to Japan and drive the 02, a completely new car. When I got there it wasn't even finished. It wouldn't fit me when I finally got in it and they ended up beating the panel behind the seat with a ball-pin hammer for about three hours to make a curve in it, so I could fit. It was all very crude indeed. I did one lap and it suffered a mechanical breakdown. Afterwards, all the F1 team managers came and had a look at it. Then they all got into a huddle, came back and said, "Tony, we're very sorry. We can't let this car race. It's too dangerous. It's too fragile. We can see so many things that will break or fall off." I said, "So was the last one. It fell apart every time I raced it."

They went away again into another huddle, came back and said that Don Nichols of Shadow had invited me to drive his spare car. I couldn't believe it. I thought they were kidding me. This was the break I'd been waiting for. Of course, Tom was the other driver, with Jean-Pierre Jarier. I went to the Shadow garage and jumped in the car. With what I said before about Tom and I being the same size I didn't have to change a thing. The seat, pedals etc… were all perfect for me. And then, what happened next, I could have cried. The Maki sponsors came across to me and said, "We're very sorry, but we can't let you drive another car." I was incredulous, why not? They said that in Japan honour was a big thing, which I knew of course. They offered to pay me twice as much as the original offer, which wasn't a big deal to be honest. I said, "Pay me nothing at all. Just let me drive that car!" They just said, "We are very, very sorry. We can't let you do it." That was the year of the torrential rain, 1976, when James Hunt won the championship. I was just spectating, and Tom of course led the race at one stage until chunks of rubber came off his tyres and caused the engine to overheat and break. One of my best specialities is wet weather driving. Who knows where I could have finished in that race? Tom and I could have been team-mates in the same F1 team.

We had so much fun. The fun seemed to go out of racing when the money and sponsorship came in. At the time of Tom's accident I think someone called me. I can't remember who, but they said, "Have you heard the terrible news?" Of course, it affected me badly. A terrible, terrible thing. The safety was awful in those days, both track-wise and the cars were far less safe. I saw so many people killed in the seventies.

I went to the memorial in Ruthin when it was unveiled, which was quite a hard thing to do. I felt I should do that. I go most years to Tom's grave, with Dave Jones. We meet up, put flowers on Tom's grave and then go for a quiet drink.

Fooling around with Tony in the driveway of Red Webb's house, where they both lodged early in their careers. **(Tony Trimmer)**

ANDY ROSS
Friend

Like many other people I first came across Tom at Motor Racing Stables, the racing school based at Brands Hatch, and when he was at Red Webb's with Tony Trimmer. Red called all her lodgers "her boys." It was just across the road from the main entrance to the circuit. The parties were magic! At one of the parties Tony had won 100 bottles of sparkling wine for winning a support race at the Grand Prix meeting. The 100 bottles kept the party going very nicely. All of us, including Tom, were popping the corks out of the bottles into the polystyrene tiles on the ceiling and leaving large dents in them. It was like a war zone. Red was seething!

Then I started my own car repair business in a barn which was used as a chicken shed on a farm next door to the Warwick Smiths, who of course were Nella's parents. One day Tom appears next door as Nella's boyfriend. I used to service Tom's MGB, which was his pride and joy. I used to do the work in exchange for the odd pit pass or circuit entrance ticket, as none of us had any money back then. That was before he got into F1. He would have been in Super Vee around that time.

On Friday evenings we used to go up to the Brands Hatch club bar and meet up with the Motor Racing Stables boys for a drink, and then go to the Red Lion in Farningham to play darts. Then it was on to the Hilltop Hotel at the top of Wrotham Hill, only a couple of miles from Brands and quite a notorious place. Sometimes Tom would be there, and one time he let the fire extinguisher off and said, "They do work then!" That was most unlike Tom. Not the sort of thing you'd expect him to do. I guess it was one shandy too many. Most drivers have to live it up a bit at times. The next day I found my green cord jacket I was wearing the night before had lost the entire colour in the sleeve where the contents of the fire extinguisher had soaked it!

He never forgot his friends from before he made it to F1. I remember sharing a bottle of champagne with him after he'd won the 100 bottles for being the fastest driver in the first official practice session for the Grand Prix at Brands.

I later moved to a garage and workshop in Sevenoaks and remember meeting him in the town and going to the Black Boy

Andy Ross remembers Tom from his Brands Hatch days, where he is pictured on the grid in his Royale RP11 awaiting the start of the Formula Three race at the 1972 John Player Victory Meeting. Tom would finish sixth that day. **(Andy Ross)**

public house. It wasn't long after the Japanese Grand Prix and the Shadow had blown its engine. "Do you know how many pieces they are in a DFV?" says Tom. "How many?" I ask. "Bloody millions! I should know, I covered the track at Fuji with that many."

We kept in touch and I went to Ightham a couple of times to see him and Nella after they were married. I even went with a friend to Watkins Glen in '75 to watch him race in the US Grand Prix.

I was at work in my garage with Nella's brother Peter, who was helping me out, when we heard that there had been an accident at Kyalami involving a British driver. Peter immediately got very upset and I said, "It can't be Tom, it must be one of the other British drivers." Then, of course, when I got home later I found out it was Tom.

PETER WILLIAMS

Childhood Friend

A new term began at Frangoch School, Denbigh, and I shared a two-seater desk with a new pupil, Maldwyn Pryce. His birthday was 11th June, and mine the 12th. He always let me know he was older than me. Neither of us were special at school. His mother sent him to Frangoch to learn English. His father was a policeman and was moved to another area, so Maldwyn eventually left the school.

Years later, when I was probably 14 years old, Maldwyn moved to 49 Bryn Stanley, Denbigh. I lived at number ten, so we became friends again. He had very few friends in Denbigh, because he was either at school or working at the weekend for a friend of the family. While I was once out walking my dog I saw Maldwyn and he told me that the job was delivering from a lorry. I'd always thought it was delivering bottles of lemonade, but someone told me that he delivered bread. With the money he earned he bought himself a first-class racing bike with five gears, while I only had a three-speed bike. He used to cycle to Nantglyn to see his friends. He was also obsessed with lorries, and could identify any lorry day or night by its lights and grille. He was always correct in his identification.

At 15 years of age it was time to leave school, and I attended the Technical College in Colwyn Bay to learn engineering. Maldwyn, who was training to be a mechanic, attended Barberry Hill College in Colwyn Bay. On Fridays I went to Barberry Hill to learn metalwork, so I would see him. By that time he was motor racing mad. At lunchtime we would walk into town, and he never stopped talking about driving a Formula One car. He could really imagine himself doing it, and would make brrm, brrm sounds and the noise of screeching tyres taking a bend. I once remember thinking to myself, Give it a rest, you will never be a Formula One driver.

He also had a soft spot for a sixth form girl from the school opposite the college. He always went red when he saw her, and was too shy to talk to her. At the same time he fancied a hairdresser, a little blonde, very smart young lady. He really wanted to know her but, like the rest of us, was too shy to speak to her.

I travelled to Colwyn Bay every day by bus, while Maldwyn lodged with a friend, Adrian Lloyd Jones, in the town. He would go back home on a Friday and go to the Nantglyn Youth Club. Friday was youth club night and nothing was more important to him than Nantglyn village and his friends. Personally, I'm surprised no one has realised how important the village and his friends were to him. His father's job moved him around, so he never had a chance to make good friends in other places.

One Friday night he twisted my arm to cycle with him to the youth club. It was okay for him with his racing bike with five gears, but not so much for me with only three. Believe me, he rode that bike like hell. It was possibly his first taste of speed? It was interesting cycling, because you talk a great deal and on one occasion he admitted to me that he wanted to be the lead singer in the band that practised at the youth club, or maybe play the guitar. I only cycled about six times to the youth club. It was his world, not mine. Sometimes his father would drive us down there.

He then went his own way, doing Formula Ford with Brian Holland. I went the other way, football and motorcycles. I watched his progress in motor racing and was pleased with his success. Unfortunately, I remember to the inch where I was standing the day

Tom displayed a desire for speed from his early days. **(Dave Jones Collection)**

my father told me of his accident and his death. It was a big shock.

What stands out in my mind about Maldwyn is, without doubt, his dream of driving a Formula One car. His visualisation of doing such a thing at 15 years old, and his determination to succeed, but most of all the value of his friends and his love of Nantglyn, which was home to him, always!

MIKE DOODSON

Journalist

I would certainly have come across Tom in his early days in SuperVee and Formula Atlantic when I was working for *Motoring News*. But, it wasn't until I went to work for *Motor* magazine in 1974 covering Formula One that I got to know him much better.

We did sit down together once, when I was asked by Gérard 'Jabby' Crombac to write a feature for the French magazine *Sport Auto*. 'Jabby' was completely knocked out by the fact that Tom couldn't speak a word of English for the first ten years or so of his life, having only conversed in his native Welsh tongue as a youngster. He couldn't come to terms with it at all. I sort of became the guy that the French journalists would look to when it came to Tom, they mistakenly thinking he only spoke Welsh. Of course, I did not speak a word of Welsh.

I remember only bits and pieces of his early races in F1. There was, of course, the business at Monaco in '74 when the Token team's entry – Tom was entered to drive for them – was refused by Bernie (Ecclestone), representing the constructors. I suspect it was because Bernie regarded Token as an amateurish operation, despite some of those involved having a respectable record outside of F1. He subsequently got a drive in the F3 race courtesy of Tony Vlassopulos, who was involved with Token, and won convincingly, which made all the F1 team managers sit up and take notice.

He certainly was a natural. He got into an F1 car and was immediately on the pace. He was going to go on to great things. I never regarded him as being dangerous. Daring, yes, but never dangerous. I don't remember anyone ever saying to me that he's too dangerous and he'll never go far. There were so many young drivers, especially then, who tended to overdo it, and you'd see them having crashes. Tom had his fair share in the first couple of seasons, especially with James Hunt. They seemed to have a magnetic attraction to each other, plus the usual incidents caused by car failures – which were quite common at that time – rather than his own mistakes.

I've heard some people say he didn't realise how good he was. I think that's underestimating him. I think he knew how good he was. He was shy. It's not as if he shouted it around the place. Unless you've got confidence in your ability you're never going to get anywhere in F1. I think to suggest he didn't have that confidence would be wrong. The fact was he was able to disguise it with being a nice guy. I still think that he had more than enough, what the Australians call 'mongrel', in him to get on and become world champion.

Most drivers going into F1 are happy to have a year or two with a lesser team because it means less pressure on them. Tom was level-headed enough to know, I'm sure, that the lessons he learnt at Shadow were going to serve him very well later on. I don't think he would have been disloyal to Shadow – he did get on very well with the people there – if only because he had signed what I am sure was a water-tight two-year contract, with shyster lawyers in attendance. I could be wrong though. After all, he had ditched his patron Chris Meek very abruptly. As loyal as he was to the team I'm confident that, if the likes of Ferrari had come along, then he would have found it difficult to turn down. The ambition would have overcome any loyalty. There was a lot more 'mongrel' in Tom than I think many people realised, both then and now. There

Tom, British GP, 1974, looking justifiably pleased with his practice performance. (Maureen Magee/Mike Jiggle)

are several drivers like that. Sebastian Vettel is one, Ronnie Peterson another. Take Mario Andretti. Everyone knows how charming and nice he is to everyone but, on the track, he was an absolute rat.

The one outstanding event that involved me personally was when we'd come back on the same flight from one of the distant fly-away races outside of Europe. We collected our

Clipping the apex at Surtees Bend at Brands Hatch in the 1974 British Grand Prix, one of the many Formula One races Mike Doodson reported on for *Motor* magazine.
(Maureen Magee/Mike Jiggle)

bags together and Tom asked me where I was going. "Back to Central London where I live" I answered. Then he asked how I was getting there. "I'll get the tube" I replied, and he said, "I've got my car outside. I'll give you a ride home." He put all my luggage in his MGB and we set off at a brisk pace, but not stupidly fast – I had the impression it was the first new car he'd ever had, so he cared for it – and he took me all the way to my basement flat in Islington. On the way I asked where he was going, and it turned out that he lived in Kent, near Brands Hatch, which was in completely the opposite direction. What he'd done, he'd generously gone completely out of his way to drop me in North London, emphasising what a nice, generous person he was. Also, I suspect, he knew it was always a good thing to stay on the right side of the press.

ALAN CORNOCK

Royale Racing

When Tom was driving a variety of Royale Cars in Formula F100, Super Vee and eventually Formula Three, I was working at Royale, mainly as a parts man and arranging car builds etc… My boss at the time, the late Bob King, was the man who fully appreciated Tom's talent as a driver and, together with MRS, made it possible for him to compete in competitive formulae.

I recall Tom being a rather reserved person out of a car, but when driving he became a totally different character. His first major success was winning the opening round of the highly competitive British Formula Three Championship at Brands Hatch in 1972, driving our then unfancied Royale RP11. This result helped kick-start our Formula Three business, resulting in the sale of a further eight cars that season. I was unfortunately unable to attend the meeting, being laid up in bed with a serious bought of 'flu, but remember the euphoria back at the factory after the event.

I also recall going with Bob to a very damp and foggy Mallory Park back in 1972 to watch Tom drive our one-off RP12 Formula Atlantic car, which brought him to the attention of the Formula One brigade. They obviously made him an offer he could not refuse and Bob, being the type of guy he was, didn't stand in his way.

There is no question in my mind that Tom's performances in our cars helped Royale to become a worldwide constructor of race cars, and that one day he would surely have become a Formula One world champion.

A page from the Royale brochure.

(Dave Jones Collection)

Posing for the camera after receiving the BP Man of the Meeting at Brands Hatch. A trophy, a rally jacket and a £10 petrol voucher were the bounty for his efforts.

(Maureen Magee/Mike Jiggle)

Tom did much to raise the profile of Royale, then owned by Bob King. Alan Cornock would take over the reins and the success continued for many years. **(Jeff Bloxham)**

TED WENTZ
Racing Driver and Friend

I first met Tom in January, 1973. I had travelled to the UK to go to the annual Racing Car Show at the recommendation of Brian Hampsheir of Elden. Danny Sullivan had finished a year living at Red Webb's house on the A20 in West Kingsdown. As I was intending to stay in England and pursue the proven path to Formula One through Formula Ford as others had done so successfully, I was going to need some digs. Danny recommended Red's as several up-and-coming drivers lived there, with the major benefit that Red's was just across the road from Brands Hatch.

Red now had a spare bed with Danny moving on to live with his girlfriend, so she agreed to take on another Yank. At the time Tom, Tony Trimmer, Jorge Koechlin and Frank O'Conner were living there. We had all come there to pursue our dreams and have an affordable roof over our heads. Red was not at all greedy and the cost of room and board was a fiver a week. She was a peach. She and her husband George were extremely knowledgeable about not only who the drivers were, but about the politics behind the scenes. Red had a strong East End accent and a wicked sense of humour. God forbid you had a high opinion of yourself and your abilities, because you would be cut down to size with due dispatch.

We all took our meals together in the morning and the evening. When I arrived, introductions were made. I knew who Tom and Tony were, as back in the States we avidly consumed *Autosport* and *Motoring News*. No doubt Tom and Tony were not too impressed with another Yank wannabe, but I found them both to be fascinating characters. Tony had a very serious demeanour, and was not prone to superficial conversation. Tom, although somewhat taciturn, had a mischievous twinkle in his eye and the hint of a wry smile. Along with his Welsh lilt it made for a very likeable persona. His Dad used to visit him at Red's from time to time. He was a big fellow, a policeman, I think. At the time Tom was becoming quite reckoned with as a future talent. Anyone who saw him drive knew it. He wasn't conceited like some of the other drivers could be, nor was he an extrovert, but he enjoyed a good joke.

Since we all lived to drive fast it was only natural that we wanted really quick road cars. Trimmer had a purple 3.0-litre Mk1 Capri, Koechlin a Mk1 Escort 1300 GT, Tom had a lovely Tahiti Blue MGB GT and I had a 1293 Cooper S. After dinner we would drive off to the local Kent pubs which graced the area, with pretty girls behind the bar. I'll never forget sitting in the passenger seat of Tom's MG late at night while we raced from one pub to the next. Narrow lanes, tall hedgerows and blind turns taken skilfully at unholy speed make for an existential experience. Mr Toad's ride wasn't nearly as wild. God how I loved it!

Also, there was a pub on one of the lanes behind Brands Hatch. I forget the name of it, but we used to go there quite a lot. I think that's where Tom met Nella, because I'm pretty sure I heard him talking to Jorge about this pretty girl that he'd met and was hoping to start seeing.

We all knew that Tom's star was on the rise. This must've caused some consternation for Tony, as I'm sure he thought it was his turn. He had been at it longer and was certainly a driver to be reckoned with. As I recall, Tom's big international break came that summer when he landed a Formula Two drive with Ron Dennis. At that point it was obvious to us that he was firmly on his way, and we were all a little envious, but proud of him. I moved out of Red's in early autumn and into a bungalow on the Downs near Maidstone. The last time I saw Tom was with Nella when they came to a birthday party that my future wife put on for me in November. We all drank too much rough cider and, from there, the mists of time start to close in. Tom deserves to be remembered. That year at Red's was quite an experience, that I'll never forget.

Working the nearside rear tyre hard – typical Tom – in the Motul M1 in one of his frequent Formula Two outings in 1973. **(James Beckett Collection)**

DAVE RICHARDS

Co-Driver

We were both local to Ruthin. I didn't know Tom school-wise, but I got to know him more when he started racing. His father was the local police sergeant, and my brothers and I were always involved in motor car incidents around the area! My youngest brother was actually arrested on his sixteenth birthday for riding his motorbike while intoxicated. Jack was a lovely guy, and we used to see him regularly. I followed what Tom was doing, and attended the British Grand Prix where he started from pole position.

Tom and I saw each other socially during that period, and I suggested to him that he come and do a rally with me some time. The problem was, with his schedule and my schedule, it wasn't very easy to find an event we could do. I was competing at the time as well. As it happened there was an event on Epynt between Christmas and New Year. I told Tom I could borrow a Lancia Stratos, which was the car of the moment, from Chequered Flag in London. Tom, Nella, my wife Karen and myself all went down and stayed the night before the rally in a little pub. We drove around some of the roads to see what they were like, because Tom didn't have much of a clue what he was letting himself in for.

We set off on the first stage and it all seemed under control to me. He wasn't used to someone in the left-hand seat telling him what to do, but he was getting there. I think we caught one car early on and got past. As we came down to a bridge the sheep had been all over the road and he left the braking rather late. We ended up over the edge and into the river. It's the only time I've ever been put in hospital by a car accident. I cut my knees on my dashboard and ended up being driven to the local hospital to have stitches put in them. The team spent the rest of the morning repairing the car, and the gravel stage at Sweet Lamb Forest in the afternoon was to be televised. We got the car going again and did that stage, which made everyone very happy as so many had come along to see Tom. We thought we better have a return go at it some time, as we saw it as unfinished business. Unfortunately, we never had the opportunity.

Whenever I was in north Wales I would go and visit Jack. I'm president of the local motor club there, and we decided to arrange a monument to Tom. We got a committee together and raised some funds for it. The monument is in a great location in Ruthin. I was there the other day with Phil Mills. We were doing a classic car rally and stayed in Ruthin the night before. I said, "C'mon Phil, we're gonna walk down the high street and I'll show you this." It's surprising the number of people who make a diversion to see it, a small pilgrimage.

Tom was very shy, and didn't shout from the heights about what he did. He just slotted in with everyone any time he came home. He was a very quiet, thoughtful person. Kyalami was one of those events where you remember exactly where you were at the time you heard about it. There are only a few things like that I can remember. I was out in Kuwait, where Karen and I had been invited to dinner. There were six or eight of us at the house. As we walked in and were offered a drink someone asked if we had heard about the terrible news in South Africa. We were so upset we couldn't stay.

My closest connection with Tom was through the rally in the Stratos. I remember following him in every Grand Prix, but it wasn't as easy to follow in those days. He flew the

Tom could be surveying the damage to the Stratos with a look like that.
(Geoff Mitchell)

flag for Wales. I'd been brought up in Wales and was very patriotic. Tom was our local hero, flying the Welsh dragon around the world.

Tom in action on the Epynt Stages rally, his first competitive outing in a rally car. **(Dave Jones Collection)**

JOHN WATSON

Racing Driver

I saw Tom racing one day at Brands Hatch in a Formula Atlantic race, and he stood out like a sore thumb above everybody else. It was a competitive series and, just visually on the race track, you could tell the kid knew what he was doing. It didn't take Einstein to work out he had a future ahead of him.

We did a race together at the Nürburgring in '75. The car was originally a John Wyer Gulf Mirage-Ford, which had been bought by a guy in Germany called Georg Loos. I ended up going off the road and that was the end of the race. Tom was a very fine driver, who unquestionably had the raw talent and skill to take him further down the road to success. Where Tom may have differed from some other hard-nosed competitors was that he was a gentle man. He wasn't aggressive and self-promoting. He promoted himself on the race track, and that was his calling card.

Tom came from rural Wales, and I come from Northern Ireland. In a similar way I was fundamentally self-effacing and very shy. I don't know if he knew his potential, or what it could ultimately lead to. Sometimes one doesn't understand that, but

other people will see it. Tom was employed because of his ability and his potential.

When Tom won the Race of Champions I finished second to him in the Surtees. I had to battle my way to the front and didn't really see him. We didn't have many on track battles. I remember a couple of times in '76 racing in a pack with him at Zandvoort and the Osterreichring, where I took my first Grand Prix victory. My observations of Tom were that he was certainly a racer. There are people who are racing drivers, and then there are people who are racers, which is what I think you should be.

Part of what attracted Tom to the Shadow team was Alan Rees. There was a synergy and a family feel which he got from Alan and his then wife, Debbie. I was very friendly with both of them. In the days when it was acceptable to go down to a rival team and sit down for a cuppa and a chat, I would be round at Shadow at least once a weekend at every event, probably. Tom and Nella would be there, and there would be the usual small talk and leg pulling. Tom was not a gregarious, James Hunt-type character. He wasn't

surrounded by millions of babes. He met Nella, they fell in love and they got married.

We were at a Formula Two race in Sicily in '74 at Enna, a circuit with a lake in the middle. There was no food at the circuit, so a group of us including Tom and Nella went off to a restaurant in a little town. I'm a bit of a foodie, and I love Italian cooking. We went there, and I'm immediately reading the menu. "Tom, what are you going to have?" "Chicken and chips," he said. "Tom, for fuck's sake! You're in Italy, in Sicily. You've got some of the finest food in the world." That's where he was maybe still the boy from Wales. He hadn't learned at that point to enjoy different cuisines. I think he did, largely due to Nella. She had come from a more sophisticated background, so she was able to help guide Tom through some of the places of life, of which food is a significant part. Tom did mature and develop as a person as he went through his career.

I was in Kyalami about three weeks ago, broadcasting at an event. It was 42 years ago but people still ask me about that race in '77. It was a horrible, horrible accident. I was on a different part of the track and didn't understand what had occurred

until the race had finished. There was a Shadow and a Ligier in the catch fencing down at Crowthorne, so I assumed there had just been a normal two-car incident. Of course, it happened right in front of the pits, with all the team personnel there. It was horrific.

I've done a number of things over the years acknowledging Tom's success and what he achieved, and I hope those programmes are contributing to a public awareness of him. I remember him as a competitive racing driver, self-effacing and principally shy, but someone who became more comfortable with his status. He was born with a natural gift, which he probably never knew he had, but it got exposed and he was then able to enjoy it. There's no doubt he needed to move on from Shadow, and maybe because he was such a nice guy he didn't want to leave the team that gave him his opportunity. For his future he was going to have to move elsewhere. I think if he had gone to Lotus in 1978 he would have been in with a chance of winning the championship, although he may have been driving under terms and conditions which were deferential to Mario (Andretti), as Ronnie

John Watson in discussion with Tom at Enna in 1974, where the Northern Irishman was frustrated by Tom's refusal to try the local cuisine. (**Jutta Fausel**)

(Peterson) did. I think, for his own development, he needed to not focus on comfort and happiness in a team, but on what was going to give him the best chance of winning races and the world championship.

I think he would ultimately, and reluctantly, have left Shadow. We'll never know what may have happened in '78 as the accident happened early in the season, before the rumour mill kicked in. The question I have, if the accident hadn't occurred, is What would Tom be doing now? I'll tell you one thing. He wouldn't be sitting down in Monte Carlo, that's for sure.

MIKE WILDS

Racing Driver

I was very friendly with Bob King of Royale. We both had a passion for flying, and Bob always spoke fondly of Tom. We didn't really get to race against each other much, but I did get to know him during my brief F1 career in 1975. I think I instigated our first conversation in an airport lounge. We talked on the 'plane to Argentina and Brazil. Every time I saw Tom in the paddock he had time for a chat. He was a very affable man. I never worked with him, but he appeared very laid back and didn't seem to get wound up.

As a driver I admired Tom greatly. If he would have been put in a Ferrari or a McLaren he would have been right up there. In Argentina it was a privilege to sit behind him and watch him do his thing, which he did very well. Ironically, I would drive that very Shadow two years later in the UK.

I think any driver who has the finesse to be as good as Tom likes the wet. The finesse you have to use to be quick in the wet is immense. Tom had it and rightfully shone. He was a quiet man, not gregarious at all, and I remember him always being very, very nice to me.

Mike Wilds, in his Dempster Engineering March, follows Tom closely during practice for the 1974 British Grand Prix at Brands Hatch. **(Grand Prix Photo/Peter Nygaard)**

DANNY SULLIVAN
Racing Driver

Tom was already well ensconced at Red Webb's place when I arrived there in early 1972. It was some place, and she was a piece of work! But, she loved it, having a house full of budding racers. I have never eaten so much beans on toast, which was a little tough.

Tom was a fantastic guy, but so quiet. He was amazing in the way he could sit in the front room with a cup of tea, reading *Autosport* and *Motoring News* over and over. I was working down the road for Eldens, chasing money etc... and he would just sit around the house. Then somebody would phone, ask him to test a car, and he'd be off and he'd end up being the quickest.

Going to the pub was something we didn't do that often. We didn't have much money, and nobody while I was there was in 'party' mode. In Tom and Tony Trimmer you didn't exactly have two big conversationalists!

Someone called him to go to the Nürburgring to race a Super Vee. He went off, and when he came back I was asking him how he got on. Was it hard to learn? You didn't have very much practice etc..., and he said, "I won. Every time there was a brow, or I

didn't know which way it went, I just drove down the middle of the road. That way, if I had to turn left or right I was part of the way in the right position." He was so matter of fact about the whole thing, and he'd never been there before!

Another memory is of an F3 race at Brands Hatch. It was a big event with all the top names, James Hunt etc..., and he just blew them all away. Afterwards, I was asking him why he just seemed to be going quicker and quicker, even though he had a big lead towards the end of the race. He said that every time he looked in the mirror he saw an STP sticker, and he knew that Hunt's car carried STP sponsorship so thought he was right behind. It turned out that the owner of the car had done a last minute deal with STP, and he was seeing the STP sticker on his own car in his mirror. Those deals were pretty common back then. You usually got a cash bonus if you won the race.

I really think, certainly from the speed perspective and talent-wise, he would definitely have been a world champion, if he'd got into the right car/team. Shadow showed a lot of speed, but I'm not sure they would

By the time Danny Sullivan first met Tom at Red Webb's in 1972, Tom was making a name for himself in Formula Three in a Royale RP11. Here he is pushing hard at the bottom of Paddock Bend at Brands Hatch. **(Peter Carey)**

have had enough to get to a higher level. Lotus, McLaren and Williams were the powerhouses at that time, so one of them would have grabbed him.

At the time I knew him he was so calm and collected. I'm not saying he was always that way internally, but outwardly he was. His demeanour was slow and methodical, nothing kinda

flustered him. He was what you would call a natural. He just went out and drove whatever it was. All he wanted to do was to drive a car, period! While I'm sure he wanted to make a living the fame and fortune never came into it. He wasn't motivated by money. Like everyone else he was trying to get into the best car and be the fastest.

TONY SOUTHGATE

Shadow Chief Designer

Tom was just this young kid that we grabbed after his impressive performance in winning the F3 race at Monaco. He just slotted in so well and never went anywhere else. A faithful lapdog! He was impressive straight away, qualifying third at Dijon in only his second race for us. A fantastic performance, and he was so easy to work with. You couldn't get rid of him, he was always there. Most drivers after practice/qualifying etc... will have a quick chat, then disappear to have a good time or what have you, but Tom would always hang around the garage, follow us around, eat with us. You would tell him to bugger off and go enjoy himself and he'd say, "I'm alright, I'd sooner be with you lads." He was just that type of chap. We were all fine with that. We were just worried he might have been missing out on something. I think he just loved being around the race cars, really. He was now in the big time, an F1 paddock, and you couldn't get any better. So, he wanted to spend as much time as possible in that environment.

He had loads of natural talent. All you had to do was give him a car that he liked and suited his style and off he'd go. It was a big step up from F3 to F1 in those days, but 'ace' drivers like Tom – and Patrese was another one – they could do that easily. It's within their capabilities. They need a little conditioning, but not much. It's surprising how quickly they find their feet. We had one of the best cars in 1975, but we often had bloody reliability problems and some crashes. Tom had his fair share of both. With a young, inexperienced driver you'd expect him to crash a bit. How do they find the limit otherwise?

He was easy to work with when testing, although he wasn't a very technical driver. He'd just tell you what the car was doing, then I'd suggest altering this or that. Then he'd go out and tell you if it had improved the car or not.

The classic testing story is from when we went to Silverstone with Tom before the British Grand Prix. I used to play around a lot with weight distribution which I would do by changing the wheelbase. I'd put a 4-inch spacer between the engine and gearbox which altered the weight distribution by two percent. I'd make a calculation whether the circuit we were racing at suited a short-wheelbase or a long-wheelbase set-up. Some circuits I couldn't make up my mind which set-up to run. Silverstone was a bit like that. The plan was to start the test with a long-wheelbase set-up and run for about 30 minutes, set a decent control time and then come into the pits. We would convert the car to the short-wheelbase set-up, keep on the same set of tyres, not changing anything else, then off he'd go again. When he went past the pits after his first flying lap Alan (Rees), who had the stopwatch, turns to me and says that he'd goofed that lap and to ignore that lap time. Next time he comes around the stopwatch says the same lap time, so Alan says, "I didn't mess up." Tom was 1.25 seconds quicker in short-wheelbase trim, which was just night and day. What it did was change the car's balance. It put a bit more weight on the back, which gave him the grip that he wanted or allowed the car to slide in a way that he wanted it to and it just suited his driving style, so 'bang', he just went for it. Everyone was gobsmacked, so we quickly put it back in the truck and didn't change a thing for the Grand Prix, knowing we had a 'hot' set-up, and he ended up on pole position.

Before then he had shown his naivety when he had asked his team-mate, Jarier, what to do at the start of the Monaco Grand Prix that year. Right up until the dying minutes of practice we had been first and second quickest, with Tom in first place. Then Niki Lauda, the bugger, went and pipped us. Tom would line up alongside him on the front row, with Jarier behind Lauda. Before the race it rained, so Tom was faced with the wet conditions and never having started from the front row of a Grand Prix before. Jarier tells him to start in second gear to cut down the wheelspin. Of course, Formula One cars don't like that and Tom's car gets bogged down, while Jarier nips through and overtakes him. Jarier did end up hitting the Armco on two or three occasions on the first couple of laps and retired. He was probably still laughing at Tom's plight. Tom told me all this afterwards. I wish he'd have asked me beforehand.

Another vivid memory from '75 is from the Nurburgring. When I wrote my autobiography a few years ago I included a photo of Tom with all four wheels off the ground at the famous German circuit. When I first saw the photo I thought 'Crikey, that looks a

Is there a finer sight? The beautiful Shadow DN5 with Tom's hand atop the steering wheel applying just the right amount of opposite lock. Car and driver in perfect harmony at Zandvoort, during the 1975 Dutch Grand Prix. **(Grand Prix Photo/Peter Nygaard)**

Tony about to discuss matters with Tom. **(Dave Jones Collection)**

bit hairy!' I know which part of the track that is, and remembered Tom telling me that he was changing gear while the car was airborne. My first thought was 'Bloody hell!' He went on to explain that, as soon as the car lands you immediately go into a hairpin corner and you have to change down, so you take the jump in fifth gear, but you need to be in third gear for the corner and don't have enough time to change gear, so you do it in mid-air, down two gears. All very matter of fact.

At the end of that year I left to go to Team Lotus on a short contract and thought Tom should have gone off to one of the big teams at that time, but because he was a loyal lapdog type he stayed. It was still a good team, but the writing was on the wall. It had started running out of money and there was no prospect of sufficient funding to develop the new car.

Jarier was incredibly naturally talented. He was generally the quicker of the two because he was more experienced and knew what to do, but he was lazy. He wasn't very technical either, just got in and drove it. Jarier hated doing the testing. Even in practice for a Grand Prix he'd do the minimum of running, then clear off back to the hotel chasing women. Whereas Tom, if there was any testing he'd be there. He just wanted to drive and

be part of the team. He regarded it as a full-time job and had work to do, which was why he was super-popular and extremely close to all the team. That was the main difference between them, Jarier wanted to be somewhere else. Just different characters really.

I can't remember which race it was, but Tom had a toothache and wouldn't go to the dentist because he was scared of them. Can you believe it? We all thought it was very funny. Eventually, it was affecting his performance, so Don (Nichols) grabbed him and marched him off to the dentist. His teeth weren't too good, he had some crummy teeth. It seemed he was always scared of the dentist, so he never got any fillings done etc... in his youth. He did have some work done later on to improve his looks, which I think was Nella's influence.

Nella was a lovely girl and always around. She's never remarried, so she's still Mrs Pryce. You have to remember they were just young kids really. To lose your husband/partner after only a few years, she was just pole-axed.

Another member of his support team was his Dad, Jack. He was a really nice chap. He was a policeman, although you would never have thought so. It must be that Welsh policemen are different! He told me that Tom learnt his trade driving a Minivan around the hills of Wales. I think he took early retirement so he could come to more races, which would have been great for him if Tom hadn't had that horrendous accident.

The accident happened right in front of me. I had moved to Team Lotus by then and was looking after Gunnar Nilsson's car. Tom had passed Gunnar a couple of laps earlier. Ironically, the other Shadow stopped directly opposite us, pulling off to the side of the track. Then a small fire started, maybe a fuel line or something. Just a few flames licking around the engine. I noticed to my right this marshal, a white bloke, with this young African lad with a fire extinguisher. There were no marshals on the opposite side to put the fire out, so the pair of them decided to run across the track. Because of the nature of the track with the brow etc... the cars were out of sight. Then two cars appeared, side by side, which were Tom and Hans Stuck. Stuck was on the inside of the track and this lad was about a couple of paces behind the first marshal and the bloke got to the other side but, unfortunately, the lad was still well and truly on the track right in line with Tom. The cars didn't move, they just went straight. Stuck went one side, and it happened so quick. The last thing you would expect would be someone on the track. It happened in like a millisecond and, 'bang', bits of bodywork all over the place, just like confetti. Tom suffered a massive, massive impact and was

killed instantly. His car kept going and I followed its path all the way down the long straight. Right at the last moment it veered right and clipped the Armco before colliding with Laffite's Ligier when he was turning into the right-hand bend at the end of the straight. Tom's car went straight on and into the bank.

It's one of those incredible, bizarre accidents. You just wonder why things like that happen. Is there somebody up there saying, "This is your time"? You just couldn't comprehend it. Racing is one of those professions that you learn not from the mistakes, but from experience.

Rather than finish on a sad note I'd rather mention the occasion when Tom and myself both got totally paralytic. People often say that he didn't drink, but boy, he did on this occasion. It was at the Shadow Christmas party at Warwick Castle. It was one of these mediaeval nights where you'd pretend to be mediaeval monks or what have you, drink out of wooden bowls, daft stuff like that. It got out of hand with the usual throwing of bread rolls, pretty rowdy stuff. God knows what the other people thought. There were about 40 of us, something like that. A very, very rowdy night. I ended up emptying a rather large, wooden salt dish over Tom's head during the aforementioned bread roll fight because I was losing out. He got

The sheer elegance of Tony Southgate's design is clearly evident and is complemented by a suitable backdrop, the Old Station Hairpin at Monte Carlo. **(Jutta Fausel)**

me back later on. I can't remember whether it was Tom or somebody else trying to get into a suit of armour at one stage. By that time the people organising it said that was enough.

We had hired a bus to take us all home. At one stage I attempted to drive the bus, which caused panic among everyone. Then about halfway to my house the bus had to stop for me to spew up. Tom was jumping all

around thinking this was hilarious. He was staying with me that night and when the bus dropped us off he spewed up walking up the driveway to my house. I had my revenge then. We let off steam a lot more then they seem to do nowadays. They all look like a bunch of miserable buggers to me. Nowadays it's far too serious. We did what the hell we liked. It was good fun.

TREFOR WILLIAMS

Friend and Tom's Best Man

One of my memories about Mald – he was christened Thomas Maldwyn Pryce, but was known to his boyhood friends as Mald – would be when a group of us – Mald, Brian Holland, Ellis Wyn Jones, and myself – met one New Year's Eve in the Farmer's Arms in Tremeirchion, which was a little village off the A55. As always, we got talking about cars and somebody mentioned a corner in St Asaph that could be taken at 50mph. Mald said you could take that corner at 60mph, so that was the challenge. "I'll go and show you",

This time the occasion is Trefor's wedding and, of course, Tom was in attendance, together with the old gang of friends. **(Trefor Williams)**

that sort of thing. Mald, along with Brian Holland in his father's Austin Cambridge, set off to try it. About an hour later they returned, and Mald had turned the car over. The only injury was to Brian's thumb, when his hand went through the smashed side window and the car landed on it.

A friend of theirs had seen the accident and brought them back to the pub. He then arranged for the car to be moved from the site. While they were doing that a police car turned up. Mald said to them, "It's okay, my Dad's a policeman." They asked who his father was and when he said it was Jack Pryce they said, "That's okay," and drove off!

The next thing was having to go home and tell his dad. We dropped him off and ran! We didn't want to face Jack. That would have happened when he was 19 or 20 years old, before he headed south to Brands Hatch.

After Mald wrecked the Austin Cambridge, which was a big family saloon, Jack, his dad, goes and buys a Ford Cortina 1600GT, which was far sportier and much faster! Unbelievable! His father was just as enthusiastic about cars as Mald was. Jack always had a car, so from a very young age Mald must have been

influenced by that. Not many people had cars in Nantglyn at that time.

When we travelled anywhere together Mald would always be the driver. He was the most awful passenger you've ever met in your life. He was terrible, absolutely terrible, although I did drive him around for about two weeks after he'd broken his leg at Monaco in '72.

He was in plaster at home, so to enable him to come around with us I took the front seat out of my Ford Anglia. Then he could sit in the back with his leg straight out, but he was still a goddam awful passenger. However, he'd still say, "This is a 60mph corner, don't brake!"

When he travelled to Nantglyn in his Minivan you could always hear him coming from about three miles away. You knew it was him straight away from the tone of the engine. Very often he had to replace the brakes. He just wore them out constantly. He had a Minivan for quite some time, and only got rid of it after he'd won the Lola Formula Ford at Silverstone because he needed a decent car to tow it with. He bought a blue 1200cc Mk1 Ford Cortina, and I fitted a towbar for him outside my house.

Trefor, looking very much the part of Best Man, while Tom and Nella are otherwise engaged. **(Trefor Williams)**

After he moved to live in the south he did not forget his friends, and always made an effort to seek us out and go for a drink in the evening. That was typical of Mald. Very modest off the track, but very focused on it.

In the days before he could drive he'd cycle to Nantglyn from Denbigh, which was about a twenty-minute ride. He'd no choice really, as there were only two buses a day back then. He always came to Nantglyn, because Friday nights were youth club night at the Church House, which was used as the village hall.

This was every Friday without fail, apart from when it was Lent when we couldn't use it. We played darts, table tennis and Mald would rehearse with the band (The Invaders). I was never in the band, you don't want to hear me sing! They were such good times. Looking back I didn't appreciate it at the time.

The group of us would visit Oulton Park to watch the major meetings, like the Gold Cup. We saw Jim Clark in his Lotus Cortina, Jack Brabham, and all the stars at that time. There would be four of us, and two would get in the boot, so only two would pay. Mald would be driving, and he would find the roughest ground to drive over while we were in the boot to go and park the car. We also enjoyed a week's holiday together on the Norfolk Broads. All this was before he started at the racing school.

When he was involved in his racing school training at Silverstone and Mallory Park we'd go along with him, a group of us. Sometimes, his father would come along. I saw him race at Oulton Park in F100, but I never saw him race in F1, which is my one big regret. Such a shame I never got to go. I was on a low wage and it was expensive.

I do remember the exact spot where his father asked me to be Mald's Best Man. I was on my way to pick up my fiancée, as she was then, and was about halfway between Nantglyn and Denbigh, when I saw Jack coming towards me, flashing his lights. We stopped and he asked me there and then. I said, "Of course I will." I was full of trepidation about it, thinking if I was good enough and would I be up to the job? Obviously, Mald had confidence in me and sent his Dad to come and ask me.

All the old group were at the wedding. Brian (Holland), Ellis (Wyn Jones) and Colin Toft. I met them there, as I was living in south Wales at the time. I suffered a problem arriving there. My Ford Escort was playing up on the motorway all the way, but managed to arrive on three cylinders.

Nella's brother, Peter, sorted out the car for me. It was a bad ignition lead. I don't remember any F1 drivers being there, and it was pretty low-key. What I do remember is Mald kneeling in the church and the price of his shoes were still on the sole! A few months later Mald, Nella, Jack and Gwyneth attended my marriage to Ceris at the Baptist Chapel in Denbigh in June '75.

I heard of his demise on the lunchtime news at 12 o'clock. I was getting ready to watch the rugby game later on. Wales were playing England in the Five Nations. I had to go and pick my wife up at 2 o'clock and remember her saying: "What's the matter with you?'

The funeral was very traumatic, obviously. I remember on the day of

Nantglyn School, circa 1955. Trefor is in the centre of the photo on the back row (striped jumper). Maldwyn is to his right on the row in front, looking straight at the camera. Colin Toft (blond with a tie, to Trefor's left) and Brian Holland (dark hair on the second row, playing with his toy) are also featured. All would remain friends into adulthood. **(Nantglyn History Project)**

the funeral I had an interview for a job in Oswestry on a newspaper and I had to decide what to do. I rang the newspaper and explained, and they said: "That's okay, come another day for the interview."

My brother worked in a motor mart in Rhuddlan, near Rhyl, and he arranged with his boss for us to borrow a Ford Granada. Ellis, Colin, Brian, myself and a chapel minister from Ruthin all went down together in this car and, like I've said, it was very traumatic. His father asked me to be a pallbearer, but I felt I couldn't do it that day. I just couldn't.

I remember Ellis agreed to do it. Sometimes, I think back and regret it. I should have done it.

We went back to Nella's parent's house for refreshments. Nella's parents were very nice people, I must say. I do remember Nella telling me that Mald's watch and wedding ring went missing after the crash. They did eventually turn up. Also, I remember her telling me about flying home from South Africa after the tragedy, saying she was in a daze. She's a lovely lady and very nice to talk too. Very well-spoken. Just a lovely person.

RICHARD PEACOCK

Racing Driver and Founder of Ty Croes Race Circuit, Anglesey

Tom lived near me up in North Wales. Unfortunately, I never met him, but he was known to people I knew. He certainly had a rapid rise to stardom. After I saw him win the Race of Champions in 1975, which he won absolutely fair and square, he became bit of inspiration to me. He was a local lad, and I was the same age. I remember thinking, if he can do it, I'm going to have a go. A couple of months afterwards I bought my first Formula Ford 1600, an elderly Merlyn, to learn the ropes.

I was fortunate enough to meet Rory Bryne, who was then at Royale. It brought about another connection with Tom, who was closely associated with the firm, obviously before Rory's time there. Here is the tragic part. Tom lost his life on the 5th March. Two weeks later at Oulton Park I win my first-ever race in a Royale and his Dad, Jack, is there. I used to have a lovely photo of me standing with the winner's garland around my neck talking to Jack, but sadly it's been lost. I've no idea what brought Jack to Oulton that day.

Over the years since that day I saw quite a lot of him. When he retired completely they bought a house down at Dinorwic Marina in Y Felinheli. We both had small boats moored down there, and we'd bump into each other and go for a drink etc... I wouldn't say I was a close friend. Sometimes, I wouldn't see him for months. Funnily enough, Jack's boat was called *Jade* and the hull was painted green. It's still in Caernarfon where I saw it a couple of months ago. We would talk about racing, and talking about Tom certainly wasn't off limits, but I would always let him start any conversation about him.

I was involved with the memorial at Ruthin, which I think is fabulous. We were really struggling to finance it. Then Dave Richards, who was from Ruthin, and was Tom's co-driver in the Chequered Flag Lancia Stratos on the Tour of Epynt Rally, came up with a brilliant idea. Dave's a very influential and switched-on guy, and said when he was chairing a meeting of the committee – of which I was a member – that he was going to give Bernie Ecclestone a ring and ask for some help. Bernie very kindly donated some FOCA passes, which were auctioned. We wound up not only raising enough

Richard Peacock, who was a member of the organising committee at the unveiling of the memorial in Ruthin in 2009. **(Dave Jones Collection)**

money for the memorial, but also had enough to give a certain amount to the council towards the maintenance. On the day of the unveiling, which Nella performed, Bernie sent us an email apologising for being unable to attend and expressing his hope the day went well.

I basically designed and developed the Ty Croes racing circuit in Anglesey, and I'm still a director. We named one of the sections The Tom Pryce Straight. We didn't want to name a corner after him, because people would have shortened it to Pryce's or something like that, and it would have been ignored. At least the straight keeps his name alive. If I hadn't had the inspiration from Tom back in seventies there wouldn't be an Anglesey circuit today. So, in a way, he's got a lot to answer for!

The Tom Pryce Memorial meeting at Ty Croes circuit, Anglesey in 2019. Tom's old Formula Three Royale RP11 and his MGB adorn the pit straight, while the assembled masses undertake a minute's applause. **(John M. Davies)**

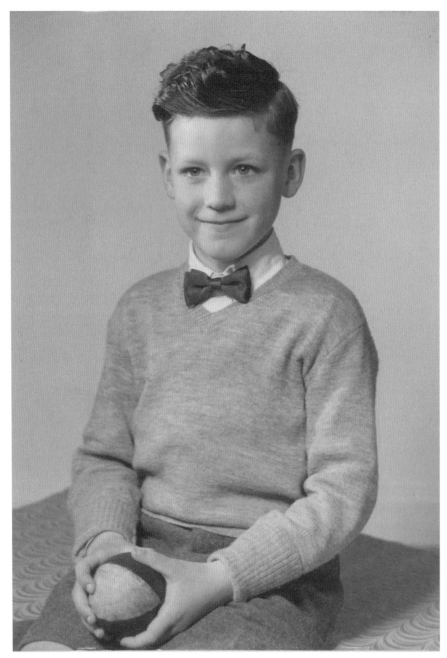

An early school photo of Tom. **(Nella Pryce)**

Another school photo, this time aged 14. **(Nella Pryce)**

Having fun at the seaside. **(Dave Jones Collection)**

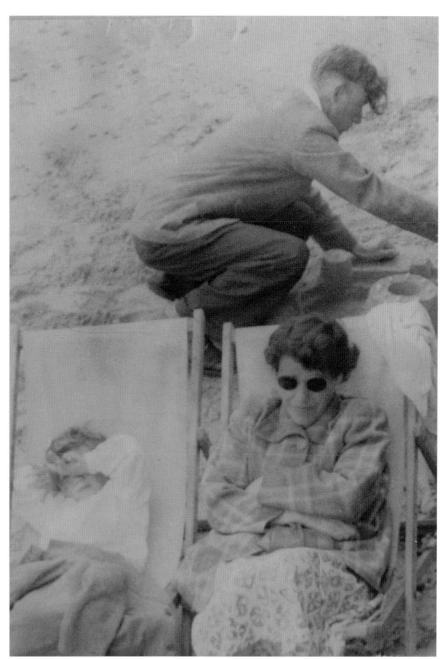

Jack looks to be having all the fun. **(Dave Jones Collection)**

You can see where Tom got his love of the outdoors and cars from. Here he is out with his dad in his MG1300, one of the many cars owned by Jack while Tom was growing up.
(Dave Jones Collection)

Jack Pryce's role was that of the rear gunner, a thankless and unenviable task.

The R.A. Osborne crew of the 75 (NZ) Squadron RAF on 28/12/44, which would have been their penultimate flight together. Sgt Jack Pryce is on the right of the back row.

Jack, second from the left, would keep in touch with his old crew – long after the ending of hostilities – who were mainly from the south of England. In the case of the pilot, Roy Alvin Osborne, he would make the trip to New Zealand in the 1990s to reminisce about old times.

With thanks to the 75 (NZ) Squadron website and Alun Jones for the above information.
Photo credit: Gerry Newey collection

Jack with Sian, at the Alwen Reservoir, Pentre Llyn Cymmer. **(Nella Pryce)**

Jack looking immaculate in his police uniform in the garden of the family home in Clocaenog, near Ruthin, with Jane the cocker spaniel. **(Dave Jones Collection)**

Mum and son pictured outside the nursing home in Old Colwyn. **(Nella Pryce)**

A young Tom with his Mum, Gwyneth, when she was a nurse. **(Nella Pryce)**

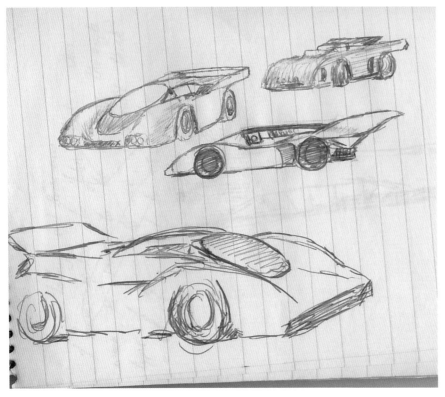

Drawings by Tom in one of his notebooks. It's no surprise that cars are involved. **(Dave Jones Collection)**

Tom clowning about with a big pipe and a bottle of, what looks like, whisky. By the looks of the weather, it might be Christmas time. **(Nella Pryce)**

Nantglyn in 2019. The house with the flat-roofed extension behind the greenhouse was the village Police Station where Tom lived and the stone building above the council houses, in the trees, was the Primary School. **(Dave Jones Collection)**

RONDEL MEMORIES

In action at the Salzburgring. **(James Beckett Collection)**

TIM SCHENKEN
Racing Driver

CLIVE WALTON
Mechanic

My only clear recollection of Tom is when he drove for Rondel Racing. Of course I knew the name, and he must have been in other races I was in. The thing is, I was the 'star' at Rondel; always had the choice of mechanics, development parts, and if there was a 'better' engine. Although my team-mates were excellent my relationship with Ron (Dennis) and Neil (Trundle) made the difference. Certainly, Norisring was a wake-up call. Tom was very quick, and a star in the making.

I was Tim Schenken's mechanic at that time, but remember Tom being a really nice guy to work with and really helpful. He used to have an MGB GT that he used to drive to the races and, if necessary, he would drive us around in it.

He was really quick when he drove for us, but he was a bit sort of naïve. It was his first time in an F2 car, but he ruffled Schenken's feathers a bit. Tim was supposed to be the number one, but Tom was certainly as quick.

They got a first and second at the Norisring, and I think Tim had to pull a bit of a stunt on him to get past. I can't remember what exactly happened. I know Tom was leading for a long time, but Tim beat him in the end.

Tom would come down to the factory now and again. He didn't live that far away. When he did come he was one of the lads, just a really nice guy.

Tom in his Rondel days at Hockenheim, enjoying the benefits of being an up-and-coming ace. **(James Beckett Collection)**

Tom, pushing hard in the Rondel Racing Formula Atlantic Motul at Croft. Perhaps a little too hard, judging by the grass in the radiator! **(Preston Anderson)**

PRESTON ANDERSON
Mechanic

I remember Tom very well, he was unlike all the other drivers I had worked for. He was very quiet and humble. He was very easy to work with. He was kind and appreciated the work that I did on his cars.

I looked after two cars for him in 1973, both were Motuls, one Formula Atlantic and the other Formula 2. Tom drove both cars so well and always impressed us with his performance.

I recall after a race, I think in Rouen, Ron Dennis suggested I travel back to the UK with Tom in his MGB GT. So we set off for the Dieppe-Newhaven ferry. On arrival back in the UK Tom suggested we have lunch at my local pub, so I took him to The Spyglass & Kettle in Wigmore where I came from. I introduced him to all the locals who were so pleased to meet a real racing driver.

Tom and his wife Nella lived in Ightham, Kent, not too far from my home. So Tom, Nella, myself and my wife at that time would go out for meals together, often ending up at my house for coffee.

I left motor racing after the closure of Embassy Racing following Graham Hill's tragic plane crash. It was a great shock to hear the news of Tom's death later in South Africa.

Tom, in action at Rouen-les-Essarts, hits the temporary polystyrene blocks put in place to slow the cars down following the fatal accident to Scotsman Gerry Birrell the previous day.

(James Beckett Collection)

JONATHAN GREAVES
Mechanic

During my time at Rondel Racing, I didn't actually work on Tom's car when he came to drive for us. I was Bob Wollek's mechanic. Obviously, with us being such a close-knit team, I did have contact with Tom and always found him a really nice guy. He was a very quiet, unassuming guy. Not too loud at all. To be honest, quite the opposite. He was very much one of the lads. Most of the drivers back then were like that, with a couple of exceptions.

In Formula Two at that time we were all a big travelling circus and very much like a big family, so we got close to the drivers, so when a driver was killed, it affected the mechanics very badly. Even when the drivers had moved on you still followed their careers.

While I look back with great fondness of that time when I thought I was doing the best job in the world, it is also tinged with sadness. I tend to look at it as a colour photograph. When I first started it was in full colour, but unfortunately with each passing year of the Seventies it turned to black and white.

A fine shot by the late Maureen Magee of Tom in the Formula Atlantic support race at the British Grand Prix at Silverstone in 1973. In a competitive field an eighth-place finish was the best he could achieve. **(Chris Walker/Kartpix/Maureen Magee)**

PAUL GOY
Mechanic

Of course, I remember Tom Pryce. He was a really, really nice bloke. He came to Rondel, I think sponsored by Chris Meek, for a drive in one of the F2 cars.

Tom was just a normal bloke who used to sit with us mechanics when we went down to the pub at lunchtime. He seemed to have a good understanding of the mechanical side of things. I remember on one occasion when Ron (Dennis), Neil (Trundle) and the other management went into the lounge part of the pub, and us mechanics into the bar, Tom followed us into the bar.

I remember Chris Meek entered him in a Formula Atlantic race at his local circuit, Croft. We fitted an Atlantic engine into his F2 car, which was pretty straightforward, and Preston Anderson, Tom's regular mechanic, and I were sent up there to look after him, with Ron driving up on race day. Typical Ron, we turned up with the full F2 truck with the huge awning etc... as Ron wanted to put on a show. Needless to say, there were great expectations – I should say assumptions – that we were going to blow off the regulars in front of Chris Meek and his entourage.

Unfortunately, that wasn't the case. I think we were only just on the pace. At one stage, Ron told us to get some of the special F2 qualifying (soft) tyres out of the truck and put them on. That wasn't strictly playing by the rules and there were rumours of a protest, but when we only qualified in ninth position, there was no need. All these years later I can't remember the race result but I recall it was quite a humbling experience.

Another memory I have is from a Goodyear tyre test at Silverstone the following year when we both had graduated to Formula One, Tom with Shadow, while I was at Team Lotus, on this occasion working on Ronnie Peterson's car. The cars were sent out individually so the driver could concentrate on tyre performance with no distractions from other cars. At the end Bert Baldwin of Goodyear who was running the test gave the OK for Ronnie and Tom to go out and 'have a play.' I can remember the two of them on opposite lock, sliding around the old Woodcote corner, which was a very fast corner in those days, side by side almost interlocking wheels. I was watching them with one of the Shadow mechanics, Laurie Gerrish, who I knew from our days at BRM. We were saying how impressive it was, but highly likely it wasn't going to end well and would probably mean a lot of work for the both of us. In the event, all ended well but I think it's fair to say Tom was more in the Ronnie mould of a driver than the much more professional Niki Lauda mould.

I spoke with Tom several times when our paths crossed in F1 and we both couldn't believe our luck to be where we were. Such a shame we lost him as I'm sure he would have been one of the greats.

At speed in the Motul at Oulton Park. **(Peter McFadyen)**

GORONWY 'GRON' STOREY JONES

Acquaintance

We were both working in the motor trade. I was working in Denbigh, while Tom was in St Asaph. I wasn't a friend as such, but our paths would cross due to our jobs. A couple of friends of his who worked with me, Colin Toft and Gwyn Evans, used to go and watch him race in Formula Ford.

The last time I saw him would have been some years later when he was sitting outside the village pub in Nantglyn with his wife. It must have been the autumn before he died. I was a motorcycle enthusiast and was out having a ride on a nice evening, when I rolled up outside the pub for a pint as you could do in those days. When I saw him I thought to myself that he wouldn't want to know me now. He was quite famous by then. Anyway, I walked towards him and immediately he says, "Hello Gron, you're not still riding those things are you?" You know, he hadn't changed at all. He was still the lad I knew when he used to drive around in a Minivan. With some people the fame seems to go to their heads, but not Tom. He definitely never changed.

Co-author Darren Banks (left) with Tom's best man, Trefor Williams, outside the Church House in Nantglyn with Tom's old MGB to complete the nostalgic scene. The Church House would be the venue for the youth club on Friday nights. A 'must' for Tom and Trefor. **(Dave Jones Collection)**

He seemed the sort of person who worked away at things. Determined, I think. He remained a country bloke and wasn't a party-goer. Such a contrast from where he lived in Nantglyn to where he ended up.

I certainly followed his career where I could. It was difficult back then, with only a few minutes here and there on the TV. Such a pity what happened. The standard of safety wasn't there then.

DAVE LUCKETT

Tom's Number 1 Mechanic at Shadow

After working for Shadow in the 1973 Can Am series I asked to go on the F1 side for the 1974 season. Originally, I was on the test car with Laurie Gerrish, but about mid-season Paul Pimlott, one of the mechanics on the race team, was involved in a serious road accident, so I was promoted to the race team. After the Monaco Grand Prix Brian (Redman) decided that F1 was too frantic for him and returned to America to race in F5000. Tom took his place, so I was now working with Roger Silman on his car. At the end of '74 Roger left, which meant for 1975 I was now number one mechanic on Tom's car, working with Jimmy Chisman initially, then latterly with Chris Jackson. We were a very small team in those days – most teams were the same – with only approximately 12 people in the travelling team. A bit different from nowadays.

My one abiding memory of Tom is that, whenever he drove, he always gave 100%, no matter how the car was. Always 100%. When you have a driver like that it makes it all worthwhile. I'm not in any way being disrespectful to Tom or myself, but we weren't the smartest people in the world. We were both learning the ropes and were both more or less the same age. What we lacked in experience and knowledge we certainly made up for with sheer effort, and a love of what we were doing. It was such a good time.

If Tom had a fault, it's that he never went in a straight line, really. Very much like Ronnie (Peterson), always sideways. The cars are totally different these days. It always makes me smile when the commentators these days say, "He's got a bit of oversteer there." It's just so small compared to what Tom and Ronnie used to have.

Tom kept asking for more steering lock. In those days you just had a sleeve on the end of the steering rack, which you machined down. I kept machining it and machining it, and in the end I said to him, "Look, you must be doing something wrong, because Jarier in the other car has only got a standard rack. You've only got half of one now." He was OK on turn-in, but he said to me that he used to take his hand off the wheel and pull the steering wheel a bit more when he was on opposite lock exiting a corner, so could he have a little more lock, please? That sums him up really.

Dave Luckett sits in the cockpit of Tom's DN5, while fellow mechanic Jimmy Chisman (left) and journalist Peter Windsor (right) appear to be deep in conversation. **(Pete Austin)**

There are so many races that stand out. Obviously, the Race of Champions victory in '75 is one. That wasn't straightforward by any means. When Tom came past the pits behind Jody Scheckter on some laps he would have a misfire, which was caused by the wiring loom being coiled around the steering column. There was nothing fancy back then, like a removable steering wheel. All you had was an ignition switch on the wheel itself. Anyway, the wires would sometimes short out and cause problems. Then, for a few laps, all would be back to normal. I do remember doing the victory lap on the tractor and trailer with all the team. At one point I turned to Tony Southgate and said, "This is easy!" What did I know!

The British Grand Prix, when he qualified on pole and led until the rain came. He was trying too hard and ended up in the catchfencing. He was lucky because the wire fence had ripped off the airbox and damaged the inlet trumpets on the engine. It was good when they stopped using catchfences.

The German Grand Prix in '75, when he had a serious fuel leak. We

One of Tom's bravest drives was in the 1975 German Grand Prix at the Nürburgring. Despite being in severe discomfort – even resorting to loosening his seatbelts to help matters – due to fuel leaking down on to his back, he soldiered on to finish in a very impressive fourth place. With typical grace he didn't make any fuss. **(Eric Lemuet Collection)**

had a dry-break coupling on the top of the fuel tank to put fuel into the car – very basic in those days with a funnel – and this was right behind the driver. During the race the dry-break unit to the fuel tank rubber seal leaked so, under braking, fuel would leak from the tank and run down the back panel of the seat. I remember wondering what was happening when Tom crossed the line, stopped the car immediately and climbed out. He stripped off the top of his suit and you could see his back was red raw. It must have been a problem for a long time, but Tom was not going to give up.

Nothing seemed to faze Tom at all. Another example was Fuji in '76, the year of the torrential rain when James Hunt won the title. When I was strapping Tom into the car for the race I noticed a problem with the monocoque, and asked him to get out. He's asking, "What's wrong?" and I'm saying, "Just get out a minute." The problem was that the aluminium monocoque was showing some distortion around the seat area. I called Tony (Southgate) over for him to have a look, and he just sort of stared at it and didn't offer any suggestions. By this time Tom was asking what was wrong. I explained to him about the distortion, and he just looked at me and said, "That's alright, the seat belts will hold me." He was so calm and collected. Looking back, the

race should never have started. We even had to drill holes in the floor of the monocoque to let the water drain out.

Alan Rees and Tom were really close. Alan had been trying to convince Don Nichols to take him for some time. Then, when Tom won the F3 support race at the Monaco Grand Prix, that was his chance. Don, being American, liked the big names. He did become a big fan of Tom's. Over the years I restored a few Shadow cars for him in California, and he would always look forward to talking about Tom.

At one point 'Reesie' tried to get Tom to calm down. To go in a straight line, so to speak, and he actually went slower. So Alan just said, "Just do what you do." Tom could get away with things with Alan, unlike the rest of us. One time we were leaving the airport to go to a circuit and Alan was driving. Tom was alongside him, and myself and Chris (Jackson) were in the back. Alan wasn't concentrating and ran into the back of a taxi. Myself and Chris looked at each other and kept quiet. Alan was called 'Beastie' in those days, because he was quite fierce. Tom was just laughing his head off, and Alan said nothing.

It was always a mad dash from the circuit to the airport to fly home, and us mechanics all thought we were racing drivers. I remember leaving the circuit in Spain and heading to

the airport. We would use the hard shoulder and anything, so we wouldn't miss the plane. I was driving one of the hire cars and was overtaking cars thinking that I had just made it, and would look in the mirror and see Tom behind me. Each time I would think he wouldn't make it this time and he was there again. We got to the airport only to find that the flight was delayed for two hours. As we waited for the flight my heart was still beating much quicker than normal when Tom put his arm on my shoulder and smiled. I knew then that I should stick to being a mechanic, as I would never make it as a racing driver.

He was very much a team player. He never seemed to lose his temper. In those days there was no such thing as political correctness so we would take the mickey out of each other and he would be part of that. He never got upset about anything.

Nella would be there all the time, and part of the team, but kept herself very much in the background. She was very shy. She would speak to members of the team, but she wasn't forward, shall we say. You could tell Tom was smitten. They were very well matched. I think, if Tom hadn't been involved in F1, he wouldn't have come forward quite so much. He was relatively shy really.

So many things keep coming back to me, like in 1975 or '76 we used to have pit stop practice competitions

between the teams. Two teams would compete against each other. To be honest, it was a complete joke. All sorts of things used to happen. One time we were up against Brabham, and Tom refused to have anything to do with it. He didn't want anything to go wrong, which of course it did. Jarier let the clutch out when the car was up on the jack. Luckily, for me, the socket on the air gun just gripped the nut and tightened it up. The chap on the other side, unfortunately, hadn't quite got the socket on and, of course, the wheel sends it flying up in the air. It was a disaster. When we got it all back to the pits Tom just looked at us and laughed his head off, then walked away. He knew he'd made the right decision not to get involved.

He was very loyal to the team. There was the occasion when Colin Chapman was very keen to do a swap for Ronnie Peterson, which would have been early '75. I think the plan was for Shadow to gain from Ronnie's experience for a season, and Tom would benefit from Lotus with all their experience. I don't know why it never happened. I remember Tom coming to me once and saying, "How do you feel about living in Norfolk?" That's all he said. He could have gone elsewhere. It's hard to say if his loyalty would have counted against him. If he'd gone to Lotus then, or a little later, the end result may have been the same anyway.

We will never know why he made such a bad start at Kyalami and was climbing back through the field when the marshal ran across the track, ironically, to help our other driver. Those days we lost a lot of drivers. Sometimes it was the car, sometimes it was other reasons. Looking back, in most cases they could have been prevented, but it just seemed part of the scene back then.

We knew he'd gone straight on at Crowthorne, but the race continued. It's amazing really. When it's serious the whole pit lane goes quiet. You just felt it wasn't good. I'm not sure if it was Pete Kerr, the chief mechanic or Alan that told me Tom had lost his life. It was a shock to the whole team.

The next day we had to pack the car up. To be honest, there wasn't that much damage. When it came back to England the car went to Pete Kerr's house and into his garage, and he stripped it there. As far as I know he destroyed the monocoque.

Obviously, when we lost Tom I didn't do the next race at Long Beach. I was back for the Spanish Grand Prix with Alan Jones. In those days you took the car down to the end of the pit lane, and Alan was fiddling about in the car. His hands were everywhere, getting used to where everything was. Don't forget, it was all new to him. He'd only driven the car at Long Beach. Once he'd left the pits I remember walking back and there

Tom in his usual pose while the usually equally sideways SuperSwede, Ronnie Peterson, appears to be suffering from understeer rather than oversteer, for once. **(Paul Kooyman)**

was Debbie Rees, Alan's wife, with Nina Rindt, and Debbie just looked at me and said, "It's not the same, is it Dave?" And I just said, "No."

Don't get me wrong about Alan, he was fantastic for the team. He brought us together. It just showed me the difference between drivers. Another difference I noticed was, when Alan came in after the installation lap, his voice was higher. Whereas, with Tom, you wouldn't know. His voice was always the same. He'd be out there, sideways and everything, and it would be exactly the same, constant.

I'm not sure when it was – it must

have been well after the accident – Jack and Gwyneth invited me to Wales for the weekend. I stayed for the weekend, and a few of their friends came around for a barbecue. All weekend we talked about Tom a great deal. It wasn't that difficult really, it was very nice. Jack would be at a lot of the races. He was just such a friendly chap, the whole team took to him. They were a very close family and Tom would go back to see them often. We always used to swap Christmas cards and so forth. There was always a connection there. I ended up spending a lot of time in America, so didn't

get to see them very often. When I stopped getting a card I thought something must have happened, and subsequently found out that Jack had passed away.

Thinking back after all these years, I think I got too involved with Tom. I was a young chap, just starting my career in motor racing. From then on you obviously still made sure you gave 100 percent to a driver, but it became more like a job, a bit detached. I kept a distance because it can happen at any time. Things were never the same again for me after we lost Tom.

BARRY BOOR
Connew F1 Team/Enthusiast

Along with many others, I was at Brands Hatch to see Tom win the Race of Champions.

The only 'different' memory that I can add is a story that came about some years after Tom was lost to us. I lived in Anglesey, north-west Wales from 1978 until 2011. For some of that time, I worked as a ceramic tiler. One day, it must have been around 1983 or '84, I went to tile a kitchen in Bangor. It's the son of the house owner who's the subject of this story. When talking to the house owner, inevitably, the chat turned to 'where are you from' etc...

It turned out that the gentlemen and his family came from the Ruthin area of north-east Wales. Immediately, I asked him if he knew about Tom Pryce. Not only did he know about him but his son had been a friend of the family, knew Tom very well and had followed his career from its beginning. He had been in his teens, I think, when Tom died and he was so devastated by the loss that I gather he never went to another motor race and had zero interest in it from that day on. A sad, but understandable story, I think.

The memorial in Ruthin. Barry Boor, once of the short-lived Connew Formula One team and life-long motorsport enthusiast, was in attendance to watch the unveiling. **(Mark Welch)**

I was very moved to have been at the memorial unveiling all those years ago.

TIM COGMAN

Fan

I was only ten when Tom was lost, but I remember the news like yesterday, and it hit me hard. Around a decade ago my brother – who worked for *Motor Sport* magazine – tipped me off that the lady who owned the cafe in Otford was only too happy to discuss memories of Tom and Nella.

One Saturday evening, after I had left the Formula Ford Festival at Brands Hatch, I drove into Otford, called the shop number and Mrs McWilliams answered. I tentatively explained who I was, and why I was calling. She happily came down, opened the door and let me in. Her husband had been a long-serving marshal at Brands, and with them living in Otford they saw Tom and Nella regularly. Mrs McWilliams described how Nella would visit the shop and stand chatting for ages, very well-mannered, polite and well-spoken. Meanwhile, Tom would stand leaning against the doorway, patiently waiting and as shy as ever.

She remembered what a lovely day the wedding was, and of overhearing a discussion after Tom's death concerning where he should be buried. She understood the family wanted him back in Wales, but Nella wished him to be laid to rest where they lived and had been married. The shop was busier than it had ever been on the morning of Tom's funeral with Jackie (Stewart), James (Hunt), Gunnar (Nilsson), numerous other drivers, team managers, mechanics and family all buying mints before the service started.

I have, of course, visited Tom's grave several times to remember and pay my respects. The cafe has changed dramatically since Mrs McWilliams' sad passing due to cancer several years ago. It sits across the pond from St Bartholomew's, where Tom lies.

(Alun Jones)

IAN PHILLIPS

Journalist

Actually, I was pretty good mates with Tom, certainly up to his F1 time. I think I was probably there when he won the *Daily Express* Crusader trophy. I got to know him through Bob King of Royale, who was a good friend of mine. When he was doing F100 I didn't report on the races, but he was on the radar. Then he came into F3 and Super Vee and was winning. I mean, the guy was just quick. He made quite a lot of mistakes, but Tom was his own man. He was very quiet and wasn't the easiest to have a lengthy conversation with.

You've got to remember that in those days an international F3 race would have two or three heats and a final, with well over 100 entries at some of them. It was a fabulous generation.

Roger Williamson had probably already matured in the category and was considered the man to beat but Tom in the unfancied Royale was in there mixing it with him and the others. I did wonder why Bob did it, he was almost a one-man-band sort of thing, but he was absolutely passionate about it. He was very

good at turning an F3 into a Super Vee, into an Atlantic or whatever it might be when it was relatively cheap to do. Tom, basically, didn't have any money at all! But, you know, it never bothered him. He never whinged about it, and because he was such a nice guy – as well as being very quick – people helped him out. Bob was absolutely terrific for him from that point of view. You'd have to say that without Bob, probably, nothing would have happened.

I remember Ron Dennis inviting me to go with him and, I think, Neil Trundle and John Hogan for a night out in Leeds hosted by Chris Meek. That was some night! Chris had bought a Motul from Ron to use in Formula Atlantic and Tom got to drive it, so that was an opportunity for Tom which he grasped with both hands, so that was the start of the next chapter.

Chris Meek was a funny bloke. He wasn't everybody's cup of tea, that's for sure. I got on with him alright but there were people at *Autosport* that didn't. The personality comparison with Tom was night and day, but at the end of the day Chris was an enthusiast and he wanted to have a go at single-seaters. He needed

A youthful Ian Phillips (standing behind the truck in the brown suit) looks for a scoop while covering the International Trophy meeting for *Autosport*.
(James Beckett Collection)

something a bit different and he bought a Motul, which Rondel had built in their second year of F2. It wasn't actually a very good car, but for Ron it was a big moment because he was actually selling a car to somebody. I really don't know how Chris met Tom. They would have been competing at similar race meetings and, I suspect, Chris just wanted to help him. I think he ultimately saw it

as a way of making money, because if he managed Tom properly he could earn a few quid, which I don't suppose he did because people weren't paid a lot in those days.

For Tom to get unpaid drives just shows you how much people were prepared to help him. Compared to today it was relatively cheap, hence the number of people who were doing the junior categories, but at the end of

Ian saw Tom race often in Formula Three and Formula Atlantic while covering the scene for *Autosport*. This time it's the Royale RP12 Formula Atlantic car. **(Pete Austin)**

the day, it still cost money, of which Tom had none. I don't think he was capable of paying. I don't think he even had the brain to think that way, to be honest. He just thought that if I turn up and do my best somebody will help me out. He sometimes tried a bit too hard and crashed quite a lot. But it was his spectacular, sideways style that caught people's attention and that he was very, very fast. Very much in the Ronnie Peterson style.

I think that F3 win at Monaco was quite unbelievable. Winning at Monaco in those days was pretty special in F3, with over 130 entries and all the things that go with Monaco F3. You'd get the French turning up with big engines and dodgy fuel. For a Brit to be able to win at Monaco in such a commanding way was just an impossible dream! I know the March was the class car at the time and Ippokampos had plenty of money, but it wasn't a great team. Coming back to F3, after a two-year break, and winning so comfortably just shows you Tom's versatility. Everything he got into he was quick. It didn't really matter what it was.

That race win certainly launched his F1 career, no doubt about it. He'd have got there in the end because people knew how good he was. I don't know why he chose to go with Shadow. Alan Rees would have been very good for Tom, not sure I could say the same about Jackie Oliver. Alan

and Tom were quite similar, both very quiet, talented and determined. And both were Welsh, which can't have done Tom any harm.

Tom did great things for Shadow and, undoubtedly, he would have won races. Whether he would have ever been a world champion I don't know. I'm not sure that he had the sort of structured brain, if you like, to put a championship together. It was more like, this is a race, I'm gonna do everything I can to win it. Winning was the only thing. Very refreshing, I must say. The thinking that to score points today might pay off later in the series was not Tom's way. He was very much there for the moment.

He was very well-liked. I don't remember anybody ever having a bad word against him. There were whispers he had a dodgy engine, his Royale was underweight, whatever. But that sort of thing was happening all the time in that era. The scrutineering was a bit of a pantomime back then to be honest, because time alone dictated that it had to be as there were so many cars to deal with. Whereas there were continuing accusations against quite a lot of people, you never got them against Tom at all. The odd complaint, but not against him. He would never have got involved with the politics of all that.

James (Hunt) was a big mate of mine. Everything was controversial

These are the sort of Formula Three grids Ian remembers fondly. This is the British Grand Prix support race at Brands Hatch in 1972. Tom leads away from pole position. There are some famous names in there. One, Master James Hunt, is partially out of shot on the outside of the front row. **(Dave Jones Collection)**

with James and he wanted to fight people. Everybody else was cheating, it wasn't fair and all the rest. With Tom, you got the complete opposite, but the difference with James was his mental capacity to work things out and win by the smallest margin. That was why James became World Champion and Tom was probably going to be recognised as one of the fastest men that ever drove an F1 car, but probably wouldn't have been a champion. I'm not saying Tom wasn't intelligent, because the moment he got in a car he could adapt to it and drive it bloody fast. Working the long

game wasn't his forte. James had more of a brain than talent, if you know what I mean.

The more I keep thinking about it, what a lovely, lovely, super-talented guy Tom was. In many ways a breath of fresh air. The thing about Tom was that he was just quick, and that's what we all liked. When he got together with Nella he was a bit more outgoing. She was a great girl. He was just a joy to watch and a joy to talk to because he didn't have a bad word to say about anybody. He just loved being a part of it. A very special guy.

ALWYN WILLIAMS

Friend

I'd see Maldwyn once a week when we were on the same course at Llandrillo College in Colwyn Bay. That would have been 1966, when we were both roughly 17 years-old. At lunchtime we'd go down to the Chinese take-away for something to eat, then call for a quick pint on the way back to college.

Every week when we all met up we'd be asking each other what we did over the weekend. Some would have been to the Winter Gardens in Llandudno, but when you asked Maldwyn he'd say he hadn't been anywhere, because he was saving his money for lessons at the racing drivers' school. I used to go with him in his Minivan. He drove it really quickly, and would always be screeching around the corners.

I once went to Silverstone to watch him race before he reached F1. We had a quick chat, but he was concentrating on his racing, so didn't have much to say. I used to follow motor racing a little bit at that time. I can't say I followed his career that closely, but if I heard his name mentioned I'd be interested. He was a lovely lad, always full of fun.

ADRIAN LLOYD JONES

Childhood Friend

Maldwyn and I lodged together with Mr and Mrs Davies in Rhos on Sea in 1964/5. We both attended Llandrillo College, where Maldwyn – as he was to me in those days – was on an agricultural mechanics' course. I was on an electrical engineering course, which meant we saw very little of each other through the day. In the evenings we mostly stayed in, like a happy family, watching the television in black and white with the Davies family. Occasionally, we would go to the cinema in the town.

I found Maldwyn easy to get on with. I think, coming from a similar village, our rural background helped. I came from Llansannan, while I believe he came from Nantglyn. He came across as a very warm person, and always seemed to be smiling. He also came across as a very confident person, who knew what he wanted, and bless him, he achieved his ambition. I'm very proud to have been a very small part of his life.

  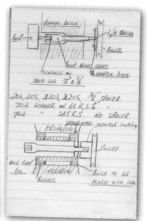

The front cover and pages from Tom's college notebook. **(Dave Jones Collection)**

RICK MORRIS

Racing Driver

In 1970 or '71 I went down to Motor Racing Stables at Brands Hatch and did four or five days with them. I had a mate with me, an American guy whose name I can't remember now. We shared a room with Tom at the famous Red's house. He was very much part of the crowd down there and I just remember thinking that he was a very pleasant Welshman.

I have a very distinct memory of his Royale association. I can't remember dates or times, but it was probably 1971 or '72. I was sitting in the Competitor's Grandstand at Brands, as we called it. The old wooden one at the top of Paddock Bend. Tom was driving either an Atlantic or F3 car for Alan (Cornock), and I remember thinking to myself, 'Bloody hell, he's going quick!' He just went quicker and quicker and quicker. He just stood out to me – a newcomer to motor racing – as someone with immense talent. I have spoken with Alan about this subsequently. It was extraordinary. I rarely ever get that feeling with drivers, and this was right at the beginning of his development. It happens

Another loyal Royale stalwart, Rick Morris - who like Tom did much to carry the Royale flag over the years - first saw him in action when he was attending the racing school at Brands Hatch. He was highly impressed. **(Peter Collins)**

occasionally, like with Derek Warwick when I was driving with him in the Hawke, and Ayrton (Senna) of course. Rarely do I get terribly impressed by drivers. Tom left an impression which is ingrained for keeps.

I also have a long association with Kyalami, in that I've raced out there for a number of years for Ian Schofield. For 10 or 12 years I was going out several times a year, leaving on a Wednesday

and coming back on a Sunday or Monday, driving Duratec/Zetec Formula Fords for him. I've been racing for about 15 years there and, obviously, every time I'm there I can't help thinking of Tom.

JOHN GENTRY
Shadow Co-Designer

I n the period when Tom was driving for Shadow, I was chained to the drawing board! Subsequently, I never got to see him race except for the Race of Champions at Brands Hatch in 1975. He started from pole and shared his 100 bottles of champagne with everyone, both race team and workshop-based personnel. I know that Alan Rees really rated Tom, always a good sign. He was sure that Tom had the potential to go to the very top. He was mega in the wet, once again, always a good sign...

He was the only Welsh driver to have won a Formula One race and also the only Welshman to lead a Formula One World Championship Grand Prix: two laps of the 1975 British Grand Prix. Tom was a fun-loving man and I will never forget when he came to one of our Shadow Christmas parties in Warwick Castle with his wife Nella, where he got up to as many 'pranks' as all of us after a few glasses of mead! In my opinion, Tom was one of the best Formula One drivers of the period, taken from us all too soon...

ROGER SILMAN
Shadow Mechanic

I remember Tom joining Shadow. You always get a feeling of what you've got very quickly. Tom was a revelation, and from the start showed tremendous talent and unbelievable speed.

I could not believe how good he was around the Nürburgring, eleventh on the grid and sixth in the race. Have you ever completed a lap there? It's frightening! He was also a very pleasant driver, a joy and very exciting to work for. What a tragic end. It was not a good period for Formula One and it's not pleasant to look back through the old *Autocourse* books.

(Chris Walker/Kartpix/Maureen Magee)

CHRIS MARSHALL

Team Owner/Entrant and Tom's Manager 1974 to '77

The opportunity for Tom to drive for me in F2 came after his dominant win in the F3 race at Monaco. It was Alan Rees who said to me that I had to get Tom into my F2 team. I had known Alan from his days with March, and considered him a close friend. Obviously, I'd heard of Tom, but didn't know him as such.

Tom came around to my house in Barnes, south-west London, and said that he would love to drive for me but he had a contract with Chris Meek which would prevent him from doing so. I asked Tom if I could have a look at the contract. He produced this document from his pocket which stated that he was under contract to Chris Meek. It was the most awful contract I had ever seen. It paid Tom a very low, nominal fee and Meek would get 15 percent of any future income for God knows how many years. At that time he had put Tom in a couple of cars, but nothing permanent.

I went over to see Chris and he took me to Cranks, a health food restaurant in the west end of London. It wasn't my sort of place at all, and I wasn't very impressed. I said that I wanted to run Tom in F2 and would like to put him under contract, but understand you've got him under contract already. I have a copy of it here and it's an awful contract, it's not fair to Tom at all. He said he didn't care, Tom had signed it and that was it. You can't have him for F2 unless you pay me a lot of money. I replied that there wasn't that sort of money available, and that he was standing in the way of Tom's progress. We parted on, shall we say, not very amicable terms. I got hold of Alan (Rees), who agreed that the contract was unfair and suggested that we just ignored it, which would put the onus on Chris to sue us and, if he chose to, he would never win. So that's what we did.

I put Tom on a retainer of £3000, which was quite a lot of money at that time. There's an interesting and amusing story of what Tom did with the £3000. Several months later my bookkeeper at the garage I owned, Ottershaw Motors in Woking, told me that a cheque for £3000 hadn't gone through the bank. The next time I saw Tom I asked him, "You know that cheque I gave you a few months ago, what happened to it?" "It's here in my pocket," he replies. "Why is it there?" I ask. "I haven't

Chris Marshall and Tom relaxing at the Salzburgring in 1974. **(Jutta Fausel)**

got a bank account and didn't know what to do with it" offers Tom. He'd never mentioned anything about it!

I ended up becoming his manager and we formed a company with my lawyer and got it registered offshore. When he got into Formula One the income tax rate in the UK at that time was very high. Most of his earnings were in dollars, so that went offshore. It was only the races in the UK, the Grand Prix and the non-championship races, that he earned

any money. This arrangement saved him a fortune, but he had no idea. Money meant absolutely nothing to him. He wasn't in it for the fame and fortune. He once said to me, "Chris, just get me a steering wheel and three pedals and I'll deal with those. You can deal with all the other stuff."

To illustrate the above point, not long after that, when he was engaged to Nella, he disappeared for three or four days. I couldn't find him anywhere, and I was leaving messages

In the stadium section of the Hockenheim circuit aboard the Baty/Ottershaw Motors Chevron B27. **(Jutta Fausel)**

for him everywhere. Eventually, he got in touch and I asked him where he'd been. He ummed and arred a bit, then says, "I've bought a house for when I get married." "What do you mean you've bought a house?" was my surprised reply.

"I gave the chap a cheque."

"Hang on a minute, you did what?"

"You gave me a cheque book and there's plenty of cheques in it, so I wrote him a cheque."

It turned out that he'd given the agent a cheque for, I think, £27,000, for an Oast House in Ightham. He could afford it with us having done the F1 deal, but Tom didn't realise he didn't have that sort of money in the UK. I asked him, quite calmly, which agent he had given the cheque to. Once he told me I rang the guy up and asked him if he still had the cheque. Once he confirmed he did I implored him not to cash it. I had to explain the whys and wherefores, which he fully understood, and I got the cheque back. I ended up arranging a mortgage for Tom based on his UK earnings. Tom never understood why he needed a mortgage.

Being behind the wheel was his domain and he was just a natural. I'd run James Hunt in F3, so I had a very good comparison. A memory typical of Tom is when we were at Mugello in the F2 Chevron. The car was understeering quite badly, and Tom was coming into the pits every four or five laps to change the tyres because he was wearing them out. Luckily for us, we had a Firestone contract, so we got free tyres. He ended up on the front row. Afterwards, people kept coming up to me and saying they couldn't believe his car control and were amazed he'd got the car around in that good a time. When I asked Tom about it, he said, "It was a little bit loose, but I had to do my best to get up the grid as far as possible." That was his attitude, always. Whatever he was driving, he'd wring its neck. He just wanted to drive anything, anywhere.

Tom and Nella were such a natural couple. I've never known a couple that was so close and so suited to each other. She was so shy and came from such a different background to Tom, but it didn't matter. She's never married again, I believe. They were such a good team. Nella's job at the circuit seemed to be to always have the kettle on for when Tom came back in after practice or whatever for a cup of tea. He drank so much of the stuff. He certainly wasn't a drinker, which was proven when he won the 100 bottles of champagne at Brands Hatch. He said to me he didn't want them, and would I like them? "Yes! I'll put it to good use," was my instant reply. I took a case back with me to London that night and ended up having a bit of a party in a

Tom, alongside the Opel Commodore, supplied by Ottershaw Motors which was owned by Chris Marshall. **(Jutta Fausel)**

restaurant. There would have been about 20 of us and everybody got a bottle of champagne and, of course, they all shook them up and it went all over the other diners. It was a memorable evening.

He had a great sense of humour, and certainly had some wit. He wasn't the sort to have been the life and soul of the party or anything like that, but he was fun to be around.

Kyalami was so tragic. Particularly annoying was the fact that the car opposite which had caught fire very briefly, and to which the marshals were running across the track to assist with, had gone out almost immediately, and the driver was out of the car as well. People have no idea of the sort of closing speed, especially with the nature of the track at that point. So unnecessary.

I suppose you could look at it another way. Tom was flat-out, doing something that he loved the most and 'bang', it's all over. He would never have known a thing about it. He was obviously going to be a big star. Unfortunately, after such a short time at the top, he was gone.

DAVID J ROBERTS
Acquaintance/Work Colleague

I first came across Maldwyn in 1965 when he was, I would think, 16 years old. I would have been 22/23 years old, and was a bread salesman working with a chap named Jack Scott. As well as being a bread salesman Jack was a Special Sergeant and was friendly with Jack Pryce, Maldwyn's father. Jack (Scott) gave Maldwyn a job as a van boy.

Maldwyn used to shunt the vans around the yard, learning to drive. At that time he hadn't been behind the wheel of a car. The first car he drove was his father's Austin A30, registration number 733 TML. He used to practice going up and down the driveway of the police station in Towyn, where his father was based. They sold the 'baby' Austin and bought a Triumph Herald. Again, I know the registration number, XUM 103. Both of these cars were black.

Maldwyn was very quiet, very reserved. He didn't say very much at all, even though we worked together. His father was a very nice fella. You wouldn't put him as a policeman. Once Maldwyn went into the racing we lost touch. He wasn't up my way very often. Jack and Gwyneth had a lovely nursing home near Ruthin,

Tom was behind the wheel at an early age. Here he poses with his Father's Triumph Herald. **(Alun Jones)**

a lovely place in a nice setting. They were both very nice people. I believe they lost another son, David, at a very young age. How tragic for them to suffer the loss of both their children.

I remember distinctly when the accident happened. Mrs Scott (Jack's wife) came into the room and gave us the news, and she broke down. The Scotts were close to Jack Pryce. I went to the

memorial service held at the bottom chapel in Ruthin. I stood outside in the street because the chapel and the vestry were packed. I remember James Hunt was one of the mourners.

KARL JONES
Racing Driver

As a young boy growing up in my hometown of Lampeter, West Wales, I can recall, as if it was yesterday, watching Tom racing in the Belgian Grand Prix on the television and thinking 'Bloody hell! A Welshman racing a Formula 1 car!' It was a super-cool Shadow at that, the DN5. Tom was always mighty spectacular behind the wheel, with such a flamboyant driving style, an abundance of oversteer and total commitment. The car wasn't a consistently winning car, but Tom was always on the limit and driving at ten-tenths, pushing the car to the extreme edge of adhesion. This certainly grabbed my attention and interest in motorsport and, of course, Tom Pryce. He soon became my hero, along with Niki Lauda. Formula One was very different back then. These drivers were the real deal, as Formula One was extremely dangerous during this period.

Unfortunately, I never had the opportunity to meet my boyhood hero, Tom. I had a dream to race myself one day but had no idea how difficult a sport it was to get into and, of course, the finance required to compete in ongoing championships.

A few years later, the national Welsh newspaper (the *Western Mail*) had a competition to follow in the footsteps of Tom Pryce and would pay for half the lessons at Motor Racing Stables, Brands Hatch. I lived almost 300 miles from there. As a child, I used to help our local milkman deliver milk, the late Edgar Davies. As he had a keen interest in rally and race cars, I persuaded him to drive me in his Avenger Tiger to Brands Hatch for the initial trial lesson in one of the racing school's Formula Ford 1600s. I was instantly hooked.

The following year I discovered that the winner of the *Western Mail* Motor Racing Stables Championship, Tim Davies, lived just a few miles away. I got in touch with him immediately, and soon I was going along with him to all the race circuits in the UK to see him compete. Now all I wanted to do was race a FF1600 myself, so on holidays I would go along to Brands Hatch and have lessons at the school. On January 5th 1979 I moved to Kent. Tim was living in digs at that time, almost directly opposite the main gate at Brands Hatch, and suggested I stay there too. I recall speaking on the phone to the landlady, Red Webb, a fiery, feisty lady from the East End of London. She tried her utmost to talk me out of not coming along to Brands Hatch and wishing to become a racing driver.

The main reason for this was Tom. He had lived there during his formative racing years and their friendship was close. Red treated all her drivers staying there as if they were her own children. She mothered us all but had a strict no-nonsense approach. She said it as it was in her Cockney accent, and always with the odd colourful word thrown in! Tom's passing really affected her, so you can imagine her feelings at the time. It was still incredibly raw when I suggested I would like to come and stay, so now Red would have two Welsh wannabe racing drivers staying with her and her family, following in the footsteps of Tom.

Red would never really speak too much about Tom, so I wouldn't ask. Over time I learned a little more about my hero. Tom certainly inspired me to chase an almost impossible dream to become a racing driver, something I had the pleasure of doing for 17 consecutive seasons, winning three championships along the way.

I have met so many wonderful people and amazing characters within the sport, but it all started 45 years ago when I first saw Tom on the television.

My wife Tina and I take flowers to Tom's grave a few times each year. He is buried near Brands Hatch and I sit nearby in the peaceful graveyard and contemplate what could have been. For sure Tom would have become the first Welsh world champion in Formula 1, no doubt of that, if not for the tragic circumstances that day at Kyalami. I am forever grateful to Tom for inspiring me to become a racing driver and also to always drive the car as Tom did, at ten tenths. Thanks for the inspiration and the memories, and I hope you are racing around the stars, with lots of oversteer.

Karl Jones with the MGB at the Tom Pryce Memorial meeting at Anglesey in 2019. Tom was an inspiration to Karl, who went on to a successful career in the sport which included a stint in the British Touring Car Championship. **(Dave Jones Collection)**

Tom had his fair share of incidents early in his career, and this one was in the SuperVee at Crystal Palace. The eagle-eyed among you will have spotted that's Brian Henton in the green car. **(Peter Carey)**

(Julian Nowell)

Off the start at Brands Hatch. **(John Dunn)**

What a fantastic photo. Just look at the rear tyre! **(Jonathan Ranger Archive)**

Another cracking shot. Same car, this time Oulton Park. **(Mike Hayward)**

Tom leads Tony Trimmer, Andy Sutcliffe, James Hunt, Colin Vandervell, Ian Ashley and the rest of a huge Formula Three field into Old Hall Corner at Oulton Park in 1972. **(Dave Jones Collection)**

Tom leads David Purley out of Shaw's Hairpin at Mallory Park. **(Jeff Bloxham)**

Chris Meek and Tom, signing the infamous contract. **(James Beckett Collection)**

The Motul M1 in Formula Atlantic trim at Oulton Park. **(Peter McFadyen)**

A one-off outing for Fred Opert, in a Chevron B27 in the Formula Atlantic race at Trois-Rivières. **(Les Amis du Grand Prix – AGP)**

A change of machinery and lots of fun, by the looks of it. Tom using the Rallycross line into Druids Corner at Brands Hatch. **(Andy Ross)**

F1 debut in the Token. **(Jeff Bloxham)**

Classic Tom, sideways in the Team Harper Chevron B27 at Hockenheim. **(Jutta Fausel)**

ALAN REES

Shadow Team Manager

first became aware of Tom's potential talent as a top racing driver during his very successful season in F3 in 1973. I remember that at the beginning of 1974 Tom started to test for a new F1 team in a completely new F1 car. Out of the blue he received an offer to drive in the Monaco F3 race, which was a supporting race to the Grand Prix in 1974. Despite driving for a team which he had not driven for before, and also a different car, he won the race against opposition from all the top European F3 drivers. Not an easy thing to do in a one-off race.

At the time I was running the American F1 team Shadow, and we needed a new driver. After the Monaco race I advised the owners of the team that we should try and sign Tom quickly, before he inevitably attracted the attention of other team owners. We signed Tom for Shadow and began a very successful three years when Tom each year gained knowledge and experience. He developed his skills and was well on the way to becoming a top driver in F1.

I remember in his second race for us, the French Grand Prix at Dijon, he achieved third place on the starting grid, and I had Niki Lauda complaining to me that Tom was using many of the kerbs all around the circuit. I took this as a compliment to Tom, coming from someone who was within a year of becoming the world champion in F1.

The next two years showed Tom gaining greater experience and good results, and he was demonstrating to everyone his tremendous natural ability, car control, determination and professionalism. His improving performances were distinguished by his victory in the Race of Champions at Brands Hatch in 1975. One of the most talented team owners and race car designers in Formula One history, Colin Chapman, wanted Tom to go and drive for Team Lotus. This interest demonstrated that Tom was well on the way to becoming one of the top Formula One drivers of the time.

My personal relationship with Tom and his wife Nella was excellent, and naturally I wanted him to stay with Shadow, which he did. Tom was always very well supported by Nella, and also his mother and father. There were many occasions when Tom's father, in particular, attended Grands Prix, and he was always welcomed

Tom formed a close bond with the Shadow team manager (and fellow Welshman), Alan Rees. **(Eric Lemuet Collection)**

wholeheartedly by all the members of the Shadow team. Nella, of course, never missed any of Tom's races.

Tom himself was very popular with all the Shadow personnel, and all of his fellow Grand Prix drivers. He was one of the nicest men in the sport, and also one of the most talented. Ever since that fateful day in South Africa in March 1977, and Tom's freak accident, I have always had deep regrets that I managed to persuade him to stay with Shadow

and not progress to such a top team like Lotus. I have always been aware since that Tom may almost certainly have gone on to be a world champion and would have probably been with us all today.

Tom's natural ability, superb car control and huge determination would undoubtedly have made him one of the top drivers in world motor racing, and at the same time he would have been one of the most popular men in the sport.

Some early impressive performances vindicated Alan's decision to push for Tom's inclusion in the team. The British Grand Prix at Brands Hatch in 1974 was just one of them.

(Eric Lemuet Collection)

DAVE JONES

Family Friend

I first met Maldwyn – he was always Maldwyn to me – through my older sister, Judith, in late 1969/early 1970, when I was 14 years old. She had started a new job as a secretary at North Wales Engineers in St Asaph, which was a local garage selling Austin and Morris cars and Massey Ferguson tractors. Maldwyn was an apprentice mechanic there, working in the agricultural/tractor department. One evening a couple of the mechanics gave Judith a lift home from work and called in to the house. After they had left she jokingly asked which one we liked best, for her to go out with. One of them was very quiet, tall and had a great sense of humour. He was named Maldwyn, and there was no doubt he got our vote. Not long after that they started dating.

At that time he was living in Ruthin with his Dad Jack, who was a police sergeant there. His Mum, Gwyneth, lived some fifteen miles away in Old Colwyn, where she ran a small nursing home. Maldwyn became a regular visitor to our home, and I would occasionally see him driving Jack's Cortina GT on his way to work when I was walking to school.

It was through Judith we heard that Maldwyn was attending a racing drivers' school – I had never heard of such a thing – on certain weekends at Mallory Park and Brands Hatch, and that he was competing in a series of races where the winner would claim a brand new Formula Ford 1600 single-seater racing car. Was I impressed! Up to that moment the only thing I knew about motor racing was from watching Grandstand on a Saturday afternoon when, very rarely, they would broadcast a Formula Three or saloon car race with Murray Walker commentating.

Maldwyn ended up winning the Formula Ford car, a Lola T200, after triumphing in the final race of the championship at Silverstone, which was run the day before the non-championship Formula One International Trophy race. The race was run in the wet, and would be one of the first occasions of him displaying his flamboyant car control in those conditions. His ability in the wet was something he would become famous for in the years ahead. Either on the Saturday night after the race or the following day Judith, Maldwyn and Jack arrived at our house complete with the winning garland and a bottle

of champagne – I can't remember if there was any still left in the bottle. Such a wonderful memory of a special day, and the wonder and excitement of what may lie ahead.

Not long after that triumph Maldwyn made the decision to leave his job as a tractor mechanic, his beloved Vale of Clwyd, and of course his mum and dad, not to mention his numerous friends, to move 'down south' and pursue a career in motor racing. He would never forget his roots, returning home at every opportunity.

To further his career Maldwyn chose to be based near Brands Hatch, and took lodgings in High Elms, London Road, West Kingsdown, which was a house directly across the road from the circuit run by a lady named Red Webb. She took Maldwyn – along with many others – under her wing and helped him in many ways during his stay there. Judith accompanied him and transferred from her job at Barclays Bank in Denbigh – she had left North Wales Engineers some months before – to a branch in Riverhead, obtaining lodgings in Sevenoaks.

By this stage I had still never seen or heard a racing car in action, so

in March 1971 my Dad and I left the Vale of Clwyd in his Vauxhall Cresta and headed for Oulton Park in Cheshire, to see Maldwyn race his Lola in a round of the BOC Formula Ford Championship. The main event was a round of the *Yellow Pages* Formula Atlantic Championship, and as we drove up to the entrance of the circuit over Bailey Bridge – at that stage there was no sight of the circuit itself or any racing cars at all – about halfway over the bridge, unbeknown to us, a couple of Formula Atlantic cars screamed towards Lodge corner. I had never heard such a wonderful sound before. It was music to my ears. The whole scene just enthralled me. The beautiful racing cars, the noise of the engines, the glamorous girls, the flash sports cars. It was all too much for me. I thought I'd died and gone to heaven.

We eventually found Maldwyn, Judith and Jack in the paddock, just in time to see Maldwyn lowering himself into his Lola wearing some slippers! I must admit I was a little confused by this!

If the Atlantic 'experience' was spine-tingling then watching the start of Maldwyn's Formula Ford race was on another level. It was a full grid of

Jack and Gwyn were immensely proud of Tom's achievements and often watched him race. They are clearly enjoying themselves on the Silverstone pit wall here, as James Hunt passes in his Hesketh. **(Dave Jones Collection)**

A lovely image of Tom from 1974, smiling and seemingly happy with life. It is how Dave Jones would prefer to remember him. **(Pete Austin)**

wannabe racing drivers, all looking sinister in their Nomex balaclavas and goggles. The track was soaked after a heavy downpour and the fire marshals were wearing what looked like tinfoil suits and astronaut helmets. With it all being so new to me I feared for Maldwyn's safety, and wished he'd never won the car!

As the flag dropped my concerns for Maldwyn escalated, if that was possible. The sight of a full grid of Formula Fords swarming towards the first corner was awesome. When he failed to appear midway through the race my anxiety went off the scale. I was very relieved to see him return to the paddock in the recovery truck after he'd suffered a problem.

A few months later we returned to Oulton Park see him racing in the new Tarmac F100 championship driving a Royale RP4 sports car. By this time Maldwyn's driving talent had been noticed by a gentleman named Tom Smith, a garage owner from Essex who ran under the TAS Racing moniker. The Lola was run by them as well and it seemed a very professional outfit, with the car, the VW van and the mechanics all resplendent in red and yellow livery. Jack was present as usual, and Gwyneth was with him this time. It was apparent that she wasn't comfortable about her son in his new career and worried constantly, but she was there to give him support.

Maldwyn was as quiet as ever, looking very chilled. He started from pole position and won the race with ease, still wearing slippers!

Maldwyn was achieving so much in such a short space of time it was evident that great things lay ahead. So much so that Bob King, the founder of Royale racing cars, chose him to drive their new works Formula 3 RP11 for the 1972 season. It would be their first Formula 3 car.

While he was busy gaining support and attention on the track he still found time to come back home with Judith on spare, non-racing weekends. He loved his mum and dad so much. They had such a special relationship. On one such weekend Judith and Maldwyn took me to watch a motorbike scrambling event. I duly sat in the back of his Dad's Cortina GT. Much to my surprise he didn't drive like I had seen him behind the wheel of the Lola or Royale, but drove in a very smooth and relaxed manner, although at one point he jokingly lowered himself into a racing position, arms outstretched, as though he was behind the wheel of his single seater.

Disappointingly, I didn't get to see him race during 1972, and in the later stages of the year Judith and Maldwyn went their separate ways. So *Motoring News* every Thursday became my only source of finding out about Maldwyn's progress up the racing ladder. By the time I got to see him race again he was in the big league, racing in the Formula Atlantic race which supported the 1973 British Grand Prix at Silverstone. Even though this was my first time at a Grand Prix, in my eyes the Formula Atlantic race was far more important. We did manage to see Maldwyn arriving in the paddock in his MGB GT. He saw us and stopped for a chat with my Dad. They spoke in Welsh to each other, while I stood there speechless, in awe of my hero.

Having witnessed his achievements at close quarters I became passionate about motor racing, single-seaters in particular. I moved to Kent from North Wales in 1974 to try and follow in his footsteps. I was 18 years old and had just finished my O-levels, with plans to start my A-levels in law in September, after the summer break. To chase my dream I moved in with Judith and her then partner, Alan, and enrolled at the SHARP Racing Drivers' school at Goodwood. Goodness knows why I chose that option, with Brands Hatch being only four miles away. Maybe it was the fact that you did your laps in a Royale PR16 Formula Ford and the chief instructors were Derek Bell and the late, great David Purley. Alan was a director of a Toyota dealership in Badgers Mount and offered me a summer job. I thought it would have been cleaning cars, but he offered me a job in sales. I was in my element. I

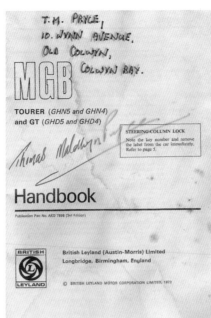
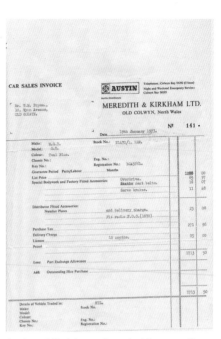

The Handbook and Sales Invoice for Tom's MGB, which was his pride and joy. Not only because he loved that type of car, but because it was a gift from his parents. That generous act encapsulates the Pryce family in a nutshell. **(Dave Jones Collection)**

was working with cars, Brands Hatch was just down the road, I was learning to be a racing driver and Maldwyn lived nearby.

I would occasionally see him at his local pub, The Rising Sun in Fawkham Green, with an attractive lady whom I later learned was Nella. I remember one particular evening I was having a drink with Andy, one of the mechanics from the garage who had long hair. Maldwyn spotted me and gave me a wave. The next evening I took my girlfriend and Maldwyn was again there. He came over to say hello, and said that he had noticed me with a long-haired lady the night before! It made for an interesting evening trying to explain that!

Another occasion was when I caught sight of him driving past the car showroom in his MGB. I quickly jumped in one of the used cars, a Toyota Celica ST, and gave chase. Within a mile or so he pulled over and we had a little chat about his progress, and my aspirations of joining him in Formula One! He did mention that he'd been looking at an E-type Jaguar and was thinking of swapping the MGB for one.

One day coming home from work I saw the MG in the driveway of Red's place, so I called in to see him. He was reading a book about Uri Geller, the famous spoon-bender!

I called on a couple of other occasions when he wasn't there, and Red always made me welcome. We would sit in the kitchen having a cup of tea and I would listen intently to her racing stories. She was a lovely lady, fiercely proud and protective of Maldwyn and, for that matter, all her other racing boys who lodged with her over the years. I can still remember all the racing stickers on the kitchen wall and the two plant holders in the front garden, which were Formula One rear tyres – they were big in the mid-Seventies!

Looking back at that time it was sheer bliss. Apart from the realisation that, after a few lessons at the racing school, I didn't have the required talent. The upside was that I'd gotten the bug and ended up staying for over a year. I never resumed my studies, something I don't regret in any way.

I followed Maldwyn's career avidly, and started compiling some scrapbooks in '72 or '73. I did work my way back to 1970, eventually. They are very detailed. I used to cut up *Autosport*, *Motoring News*, anything I could find really. I have missed some race reports, but not many. In some ways I find the early years more enjoyable than his days in Formula One. It was more real, closer to home

if you like, racing in this country in F3 and Atlantic. You had more chance to go and watch him. When he got into F1 I rang him just to congratulate him and had a brief conversation about the fact that he wouldn't be racing much in the UK any more, to which he said, "That's something I hadn't thought of." He seemed very cool and relaxed as ever.

The first Grand Prix I saw him compete in was at Brands Hatch in 1974. To think, inside that helmet, driving the number 16 Shadow, was Maldwyn Pryce from Nantglyn, North Wales. Seeing him there was quite surreal, really. To think that the quietly spoken young man I knew was racing among such illustrious

names was just amazing. It was hard to believe, and still is to this day. To have started racing at 20 years old in Formula Ford 1600 and to reach the pinnacle, Formula One, in four years was just incredible.

The following year I saw him win the Race of Champions at his beloved Brands Hatch, and lead the British Grand Prix at Silverstone for three laps after claiming pole position. Every race report you read seemed to have a mention of something special he'd done. Particularly if it was wet, when the reporters would go into overdrive. He was something special in those conditions, where his abundance of natural ability came to the fore.

Then came Kyalami. I've talked to many, many people about Maldwyn over the years, and everyone, and I mean everyone, remembers where they were and what they were doing that day when they heard the news. I know I can. I had come home from work for some lunch. My dad was cleaning the windows and my brother was in the bath. I went into the lounge and switched the TV on. It was getting close to one o'clock. I'm not sure if it was a newsflash or the first item on the news which began with, "Tragic news from South Africa." As he was saying it I remember thinking, "Not Maldwyn, please not Maldwyn. Not out of all those 26, not Maldwyn." Then the

words, "Tom Pryce." Shattering, just shattering. I do know for sure that, on the fifth of March 1977, lives were changed forever. To have crashed through his own fault, then... but for that to happen. It was so bizarre, even to the degree it was his team-mate that had broken down. The split second of it all, the chain of events, hitting his helmet etc... It was just... unbelievable. I went to the funeral with my dad and brother. A terribly sad day.

I was very fortunate and privileged to become close friends with his Mum and Dad, Gwyn and Jack. In particular with Jack I shared some wonderful hours over the years. He was a unique human being, considering what he'd been through. Probably one of the nicest people I've ever met. Such a lovely man, a joy to be with. Very intelligent, caring, funny and interesting.

We would visit Maldwyn's grave in Otford at least twice a year, always on the 11th June, his birthday. In the early days we would occasionally go through London and call and see Nella in Fulham, where she had an antique shop with Janet Brise, Tony's widow. Nella was very close to Jack and Gwyn, and kept in close contact with them after Maldwyn's passing. I'm sure Maldwyn was equally as close to Nella's mum and dad.

One of Jack's prized possessions was a photo of Maldwyn airborne at

Tom behind the wheel of his MGB, driving through the Silverstone paddock.
(Dave Jones Collection)

the Nurburgring in the DN8, given to him and Gwyn by the Shadow mechanics. It's a wonderful photo. He loved to talk about Maldwyn, and would tell me stories of the time they spent together, whether back home in North Wales or at the races. The saddest and most poignant is when Jack told me of the last time he saw Maldwyn. It would have been January or February 1977 and he'd come up to see them. He'd had trouble with his Opel Commodore on the way up, so instead of risking it on the way back Jack told him to put it in the garage and he'd take him to Rhyl station to get the train home. Jack helped him put his case on the train, shut the door, and as the train pulled away Maldwyn had his head out of the window and they were waving to each other. Upon leaving the station the train veered to the right, but with him being on the left-hand side they continued to wave to each other right up until the train was out of sight. That was the last image Jack had of seeing his son.

Jack told me that, when they lived in Denbigh, Maldwyn was attending Technical College in Colwyn Bay. Jack used to say that they always knew when he was getting close to home because their dog, Sian, a black Labrador, could recognise from a fair distance the tone of the engine of the Minivan – Maldwyn's first car – especially the way he drove it!

Another amusing tale Jack told me was about two traffic patrol colleagues of his, who were driving early one morning from Denbigh to Ruthin. The road was relatively quiet, as they were back then. When they approached a nasty set of corners, called Bachymbyd Bends, they saw, all of a sudden and out of nowhere, a Morris Oxford coming at great speed around one of the corners on two wheels. In a split second it had gone. They just looked at each other and one of them remarked that it could only have been one person who could drive a Morris Oxford like that. Of course, it was Maldwyn behind the wheel of his Dad's car. To get a Morris Oxford on two wheels and keep it there took some doing. It was a big old bus. This would have been before Maldwyn moved down south.

Jack said that Maldwyn was always watching the way he drove, and one time when they were out in his MG1300 he remembered Maldwyn saying, "If you keep revving it like that, you'll bust the engine." Jack said to him, "Don't be daft, it will be okay." A few days later the engine expired!

One of his best racing stories concerns the first time Maldwyn tested for Shadow. He'd gone to Silverstone and Maldwyn was driving around, getting used to the car. After several laps he came into the pits and asked the mechanics to adjust the rear wing. They started work with

One of the highlights of Dave Jones' life was being present the day Tom became the first Welshman to win a Formula One event. Like his countryman, Dave was one very proud Welshman that day. **(Dave Jones Collection)**

their spanners underneath the wing and gave him the thumbs up, once the work had been completed. He left the pits and was the only car on the circuit at the time. When he was approaching Woodcote for the first time you could hear him ease off, enter the pit lane and come slowly towards the waiting mechanics. Jack said that he could see that Maldwyn had a beaming smile on his face. He came to a stop, lifted the visor on his helmet and said to the mechanics, "You didn't do anything, did you?"

Another racing related tale was when Jack was on duty in Ruthin and he was walking down one of the streets. All of a sudden the butcher came out of his shop and shouted to him that Maldwyn was fastest in practice, with Jack thinking straight

away that it must have been wet, which turned out to be the case.

Then there was the time Dave Richards, who was in charge of the BAR F1 team, invited Jack to Silverstone when they were testing. Obviously, Jack had a little history with him, when Dave had co-driven for Maldwyn on the Tour of Epynt in the Lancia Stratos. Jack said he'd had a wonderful day, both at the test and when he was shown around the factory in Banbury. I remember him saying that Jacques Villeneuve, who was testing that day, would disappear straight back into the motorhome when he'd got out of the car, and would only appear to resume the test.

I always tried to involve Jack in things. He was still young at heart, so we just did things. Years ago I was having flying lessons and asked him if he'd like to come and have a go. "I'd love to," was his quick response. I took him to Hawarden Flying Club for a trial lesson and, I think, within ten hours he went solo. It took me twelve hours! He was a born flyer. I knew he had been a rear gunner in a Lancaster bomber during the Second World War - a thankless job - so he'd had experience of being in the air, but that was the first time at the controls. I remember reading somewhere Maldwyn had wanted to be a pilot, but he didn't think he was clever enough. When Maldwyn lived in Towyn when he was ten or eleven years old he joined the ACC Training corps in Rhyl.

Jack was a real car enthusiast. I was in the motor trade and, if we had a new model in, I'd take it around for him to see what he thought of it. He didn't stay away from the racing circuits. We'd go to Oulton Park quite often. It was lovely listening to his stories of when he was young. We'd talk about life in general. We had similar interests.

He was also such a generous man. I was in his garage with him one day when he gave me a blue plastic tray and told me that Maldwyn used to use it when he raced in Formula Ford. I still have it. Value-wise it's worthless, but to me it's priceless.

That's nothing to the time I came into the possession of Maldwyn's

MGB GT. There's a lovely story of how Maldwyn came to own the MGB in the first place. When he was racing in FF, F100 and Super Vee for Tom Smith (TAS Racing) Maldwyn didn't own a car, so Tom – who owned a garage – would lend him whatever he had in at the time to come back home. He came home in a left-hand drive Fiat on one occasion. In early 1973 Maldwyn had come home for the weekend, and had gone to see his mum in Old Colwyn at the nursing home. At some stage in the day Gwyn suggested they went for a walk. Not long into the walk they went past M&K Garage and Gwyn pointed to a car parked outside the showroom. "That's a nice-looking car Maldwyn. What do you think?" "It certainly is," replied Maldwyn. Then Gwyn told him she'd bought it for him. What a lovely thing to do. Maldwyn absolutely loved that car, it was so precious to him.

Initially, it seemed he took very good care of the car, not driving it in his usual foot flat to the boards style. This was evident when he was on his way to one of the races and was following Tim Schenken, who had a Porsche 911 at the time. It was when they were racing for Rondel in F2. Normally they would be doing what racing drivers do, but back then (older readers will remember) you had to run cars in, and you were advised not to exceed, say, 50mph. So, on this

occasion, he treated the car with great care and pootled around.

That wasn't always the case according to Jack, who told me of an occasion when Maldwyn came home to Ruthin in the MG and they were on their way to see Gwyn at the nursing home. This was something they did quite often. On the way there's a huge roundabout in Abergele, and Maldwyn was going around the roundabout lifting the inside front wheel a few inches off the ground. Then he'd lower it, then lift it again, all done with throttle control. He knew just how to do it and made it look easy. Believe me, it's not. I've tried it.

Jack and Gwyn had kept the car after Maldwyn's accident and used it regularly, Gwyn especially. At that time Jack had a Range Rover, and I think they wanted something more modern with power steering for Gwyn, so they bought a VW Polo. I couldn't believe it when they said they wanted me to have the car. It came right out of the blue. Jack knew how much I thought of Maldwyn. I've got a letter somewhere that he wrote, just to state that he was passing the car on to me. It typifies the sort of people they were. To be gifted such a thing is mind-boggling really. All of this occurred in 2001 and is, of course, very special to me. Very special. I regard myself as the car's custodian really. It's important to me that the

car is in good condition, because I want to keep it going forever if I can. Apart from being a beautiful car, it's whose it was. I wish I never had the car to be honest, because that would mean Maldwyn was still alive, but for the saddest of reasons I have.

I think my son or daughter will have it eventually. I did ask them a few years ago and neither of them wanted it, because it would be too much of a responsibility, but now I think their view has changed and they will most probably keep it. Another thing is, they idolised Jack and Gwyn. I'd take them with me when they were young to see them every Friday night. Other nights as well, but always on a Friday. Jack would make us all laugh with his tales of when he was a young man in the Cerrig y Drudion Home Guard, and his time in the police. It was always fun to go there.

It's strange, but I remember the MGB GT model being launched and thinking what a lovely car it was. They later introduced a new colour named Teal Blue, which was my favourite. The very first day I saw my/Maldwyn's car was when I was walking alongside the A525 Ruthin Road and there, coming towards me, was a Teal Blue MGB GT with Maldwyn behind the wheel. I thought, "Wow! Maldwyn's got a new car and it's an MGB GT and it's in Teal Blue." I couldn't believe my eyes.

Gwyn, like Jack, had a great

sense of humour, which was no doubt where Maldwyn got his from. Jack and Gwyn were great together, but different. Gwyn was a very determined lady and stood no nonsense. She wanted a job done properly, very much in the style of an old matron. At that time the wife of a policeman was supposed to be at the police house to answer the phone etc.., and wasn't allowed to have a job. The chief inspector rang one day and more or less said she couldn't work, but Gwyn wasn't having any of it. She got herself a job as a nurse at the Denbigh Mental Hospital. From there she got really fired up about wanting a nursing home and went to the bank to get a loan. When she first set it up she had nothing, and when all the rooms were full she would sleep in a sun lounger in a bathroom. She worked flat out and was very successful, which is how she came about being able to buy the MG for Maldwyn, and help him in other ways.

I often think of Jack and Gwyn and the sadness they endured in their lives after losing both of their sons, David and Maldwyn. Goodness knows what it must have been like losing both your children. I can't begin to imagine. The horror of that experience, and yet they had such a positive attitude to life and were fun people to be with.

Jack passed away on March 7th 2007, aged 82, thirty years and two days after Maldwyn. He missed out

on seeing the unveiling of the memorial in Ruthin on the June 11th 2009, which would have been Maldwyn's 60th birthday. I know he would have been so proud. At least Gwyn was still with us to be there that day, and got to see the turn-out. Nella was there and looked after Gwyn. My abiding memory of the day is when we were all gathered around waiting for the unveiling, and all of a sudden around the corner walked a policeman – a sergeant in full uniform, looking very smart, and in my eyes that was Jack. It was a fitting sight.

While I obviously remember his on-track exploits it's more the non-racing memories of Maldwyn, and the sort of person he was, that mean the most to me. His love of his mum and dad was obvious to see from the number of times – pretty much at every opportunity – he would come and visit them. His love of being back among the people he grew up with is typified with the asking of his childhood friend, Trefor Williams, to be his best man. He'd been in Formula One for about a year by then, so could have asked anyone really. Other people would have had asked someone famous, which would have been easier, but he wanted the lad that he grew up with in Nantglyn to undertake such an important

Jack behind the controls while learning to fly at the invitation of Dave Jones. He took to it like a duck to water. **(Dave Jones Collection)**

role. That speaks volumes for their friendship and what he thought of Trefor. It shows you how important the people were to him back home.

Then there was his mischievous, subtle sense of humour. Jack told me an amusing story of when Maldwyn was racing in Formula Ford and, on one occasion he'd gone to Brands Hatch to watch him. When he arrived a driver friend of Maldwyn's had approached him and asked him in English, "How are you Mr Pryce?", to which Jack replied, "I'm okay, thank you." Then he said, in Welsh, "Twll din pob sais." Apparently, the friend had asked Maldwyn to teach him a Welsh phrase, so the next time he saw Jack he could converse with him. The problem was, for a laugh, the

phrase that Maldwyn had taught him, translated means, "All English people are arseholes."

I've always tried to keep his memory alive, and to tell anyone who asks of his achievements and what he was like as a person. He should not be forgotten. I think that era suited him. Today's Formula One, especially the interviews at the end, no way! In some ways I wish he hadn't gone racing. That way he might still be with us, but he died doing something he was both very talented at and loved doing. He will live long, not just in my memory, but in all the people fortunate enough to have known him or who followed his rapid climb from tractor mechanic to one of the top ten Grand Prix drivers in the world.

MARTIN WEBB

Red Webb's Son

Tom arrived at our house in mid-1970 after he'd won the Crusader Championship. The prize was a Lola Formula Ford. I would have been 10 years old. He was an extremely quiet lad. He brought a girlfriend, Judith, with him, but she didn't live with us. He was so unlike a lot of the drivers we had stay with us. For instance, when Tom first came we had Danny (Sullivan), who was quiet but liked the publicity. Tony (Trimmer) was also quiet, but was more outgoing than Tom. Whereas the others would go over the road to the bar at Brands Hatch on Friday and Saturday evenings, Tom didn't seem interested. He seemed to really like being in a family environment.

From very early on when Tom arrived it was obvious that there was a certain, not jealousy, but a certain amount of distance between him and the others. They were still all very good friends. They would support each other and would be like one big family with us. You could definitely tell that Danny came from a different background, his parents were very wealthy. Same goes for Jorge Koechlin. At one stage his father was

president of Peru, I believe. There seemed to be a certain pecking order. I sensed that there was a certain stand-offishness with him. It wasn't because they disliked him, it was that they respected him. All the other drivers recognised that Tom would be the one that was going to come through. When other drivers recognise that sort of talent it shows you how special they are.

In the early days he wasn't particularly good at setting the car up. It was pretty obvious, not to me, but to some other people. On one occasion I remember Tony (Trimmer) - I think he was in F3 at the time - watching from the back of the grandstand at Brands Hatch with a pair of binoculars, and then telling him how to set the car up. Tony's approach was totally different, a totally different driver. Tom's approach was more seat-of-the-pants. They both got on very well, they were good friends.

He got noticed very quickly. It was quite strange because whereas a lot of the other drivers took a long time to work their way through and up the ladder, Tom got noticed very, very quickly. He got picked

The black Shadow and five black stripes on Tom's helmet would become one of the most iconic images of 1970s Grand Prix racing. **(Tim Marshall)**

up by Bob King and would race anything Bob put at his disposal. Super Vee, F3, Atlantic, sometimes at the same meeting.

He never won an awful lot of races and didn't seem to concentrate on a particular championship, but he did win some important races when the right people were watching, the win at Monaco being the stand-out. Afterwards, I remember we were getting phone calls at the house from

Colin Chapman, Don Nichols, Ken Tyrrell and all these different people, and he wouldn't answer the phone! I remember my mum would answer it. She knew Frank Williams, Ken Tyrrell and some of the others. I remember Tom just sitting back and really not wanting to talk to anyone, because he didn't know what to do.

I remember his early Grand Prix appearances. He seemed to spend a lot of time getting involved with

James Hunt. Tom didn't take to James. Chalk and cheese as people. He didn't like him mainly due to his lifestyle.

Throughout his stay with us you would never know what had happened at the meeting when he came home. The other drivers you could, but not Tom. It would just be a shrug and that was it. He would sit down, have his dinner and watch television.

I guess my memories are a lot different from the likes of Tony and the others, and that because of my age, there are certain things I wasn't allowed to see and hear. My overriding memories are not so much the racing, but of Tom spending time with me at home.

I always thought that you would never have guessed Tom was a racing driver. He was more like a lad who lived in the village, who you would have thought would have been the local carpenter or a painter and decorator or something like that. He didn't have that swagger most drivers have. They seem a bit full of themselves. Not Tom. Very nondescript, quite unassuming.

In the winter when he wasn't racing he'd take me fishing, something he still did even when he was in F1. When I was playing football, rather than my mum do it, he'd take me in his little blue MGB and scare the crap out of me!

He'd play in the garden with me, playing football, and one time – I have a photo somewhere – we used to have a little car in the garden, a pedal car sort of thing. We were going to have a race, myself, Tom and another driver. Tom was sitting on a little trike with a silly hat on and something sticking out of his mouth. We had a dog and we'd go for long walks. Many times he would just go off on his own with the dog and be gone for hours. He was such a gentle, caring person. Those sorts of things are what I remember most about Tom. Silly, everyday things.

Then, of course, there's his embarrassing dancing skills and the copious intake of tea. He drank gallons of the stuff. You would always see him wandering backwards and forwards from the kitchen, making a cup of tea, and he had his own cup. No one was allowed to use it. Very rarely you'd see Tom with a beer, but always a cup of tea, whereas Tony and the others liked a beer.

On the rare occasions you did see Tom with a beer it was usually at the big parties my mum used to throw at home. They were usually after one of the big meetings and we'd have the likes of Graham Hill and Jackie Stewart show up. There would be up to 150 people turn up. Because he didn't drink, when he did he would make a bit of a clown of himself. His dancing wasn't particularly good

Tom leads the Formula Three pack through Paddock Hill Bend at Brands Hatch in 1972. By this time he was already making a name for himself. When returning to Red Webb's (Martin's mum) he would be brought back down to earth. **(Peter Carey)**

and that's being polite. You have to remember I was very young, but even then it was different!

He used to go back home to Wales frequently. He'd just disappear off. I went with him four or five times. Sometimes, I'd take the day off school if necessary. If he had a spare day he'd just go off to see his mum and dad, back to the normal life he missed. He didn't really like the motor racing lifestyle. He'd go there and back in a day, which the way Tom drove wasn't that difficult. I've heard people say it's a four-and-a-half-hour journey,

and Tom would do it in three and a half. Less than that, if you ask me. I remember him getting banned. He got caught using the hard shoulder doing about 100mph, trying to avoid a traffic jam when he was on the way up to the Shadow factory.

He lived with us even when he was engaged to Nella, and they had bought a house in Ightham. He only moved out when he got married. Tom was just an ordinary guy who really came to life when he was behind the wheel of a car. He was like a big brother to me and I still miss him.

TONY VLASSOPOLUS

Team Owner

I guess we got Tom going in F1 with Token and then, after he won at Monaco for us, it was crazy. I still have a vivid memory of the euphoria after the race, with people sticking things on the car, taking pictures etc... and just how calm Tom was. I asked him what happened at the start and, at first, he didn't reply. Then when I asked him again, he just said he'd missed a gear! Like I said, so calm, no fuss. I remember Murray Walker saying it was one of the best drives he'd ever seen in his life.

When I was involved with Rondel Racing we had so many drivers come through. Carlos Reutemann, Tim Schenken, Bob Wollek, Henri Pescarolo, Graham Hill, Ronnie Peterson and many more. I liked Ronnie, although he didn't drive for us that much. Ronnie would be the nearest person I would liken Tom to. Out of the car quiet as a mouse, but once in the car they were off. Both lovely men, with beautiful ladies in their life.

I drove with Ronnie. Not on a track, just to and from circuits. When you drive with people like that it's so natural, and Tom was one of them. People have often asked me what

All hands on deck to get the car finished in time for practice. **(James Beckett Collection)**

makes a good racing driver? Very simply, whereas we have good vision and see so much ahead of us, these people are so much further on than that. They don't panic. If someone jumps out on me I'm gripping the wheel. But those two, it was just natural. They had so much time to react. They were a breed apart. If he'd survived, he would have been a world champion, for sure. An absolute tragedy what happened to him.

BUZZ BUZAGLO

Racing Driver

Even though Tom took my F3 drive at the prestigious Monaco Grand Prix support race I've never begrudged him the opportunity at all. It wasn't his decision, it was Tony Vlassopulos who told me of his plans on the Monday before the event.

I didn't take the news well. Pretty heartbroken, to be honest. I was excited about my prospects having been promised a 'special' engine from John Reed at Holbay – I'd been having some engine problems earlier in the season and they wanted to make it up to me – plus, Neil (Trundle) and Ray (Jessop) had dome some modifications to the car.

A small consolation was living it up with my then girlfriend in Monaco for the whole weekend, having been flown down there in Ken Grob's (Tony V's business partner) Learjet. I watched Tom win from the balcony of the hotel. He absolutely blitzed them. I went down afterwards to congratulate him and the mechanics. One of them said, "Look at the rev counter, he's used all of those extra revs." It was up at 9000rpm. At least my car won.

The car that Buzz should have driven at Monaco in 1974. Instead, it played a key part in launching Tom's career.
(James Beckett Collection)

Thinking back now, Tom did me a favour getting my drive. I was on the outer limits of my ability and if I'd carried on I might have hurt myself or even worse. Let's face it, in that era so many drivers were killed. At least I'm still here talking to you, unlike poor Tom. When I heard of his dreadful accident, it broke my heart.

TREVOR FOSTER

Shadow Mechanic

I've quite a few memories of Tom, some vivid, even though it's a long time ago. I've been spending a fair bit of time on aeroplanes and trains recently, and have been thinking a lot about those times.

The opportunity for Tom to drive for Shadow came about after the tragic death of Peter Revson, ironically at Kyalami in 1974, during testing for the upcoming South African Grand Prix, which hit our relatively young and small team hard. Brian Redman had taken Peter's place initially, but with all due respect to Brian, he was coming towards the end of his front-line career. He knew he was a stand-in, and he wasn't about to launch his F1 career.

The Monaco Grand Prix in '74 was Brian's last outing for the team which was, of course, the year when Tom annihilated the opposition in the F3 support race. I remember watching the F3 race with Alan Rees, the Shadow team manager. We'd heard of Tom, along with the likes of Roger Williamson and Tony Brise, who were all great British talents. In my view Tom was a little bit under the radar. He hadn't been competing in F3 for a while, mainly due to budgetary reasons. To come back to F3 and put

in that sort of performance was phenomenal, a real eye-opening experience. It's one of those races where you are watching and you see the leader come around and wonder what's happened to everybody else. Once in his stride he just took off like a scalded cat. The only way he was going to lose was by making a mistake. Of course, he didn't. He just kept pressing on for lap after lap. This obviously caught the eye of not just Alan, but all the Shadow senior management who were going to try very hard to get him in the car, but would face opposition from other very interested teams.

Being a mechanic I wasn't at the level of the senior management, but we were a small, relatively close team, so you could talk to them about those sort of things and they'd be very interested in your views. In those days, unlike today in my opinion, F1 team principals knew who was the next hotshoe in F3 or Formula Ford and they would keep an eye on them. Alan, I'm sure due to the slight Welsh connection, was very keen to get Tom on board, but obviously, other team personnel would be part of the decision-making process.

I remember Tom coming to the factory for a seat fitting and he seemed just a very, very normal guy. He was a hit with the team right from the first day he arrived. Very quiet, almost embarrassed to the point of thinking 'Why am I here?', but deep down he had an inner confidence that he knew he could drive an F1 car. It was a big step in those days from an F3 car with something like 130 to 140bhp to the 475 to 500bhp of an F1 car.

The first time he tested the car was at Silverstone and you knew, right from the off, he was just on it! I've worked with a lot of drivers in my career, and some – and Tom's one of them – show no nerves when you first put them in the car. They are not overawed. Within ten laps or so they're in the pits saying the engine's lost some power compared to when I first drove it, that sort of thing. I'd say within his first five laps that day Tom was on top of the car. He made the step up without even a blink. To emphasise my point, a vivid memory of that day is standing in the old pits at Silverstone and you'd hear them coming into Woodcote corner which was one of those 'Is it flat?' sort of corners? A real test. This was before

How the many people who came into contact with Tom remember him.
(Maureen Magee/Mike Jiggle)

the chicane was installed. The first lap everyone would have a slight lift. Then the next three or four laps, even on new tyres, some would still be lifting off or feathering the throttle. But with Tom, the throttle was nailed to the floor, absolutely nailed! If the back slid out a little bit, he'd just control it. Total confidence in his own ability when he was in the car.

Another good thing about Tom was, when he drove, he was aggressive with the car but wasn't hard on the

In only his second outing for Shadow in the French Grand Prix in 1974 at Dijon-Prenois, Tom qualified an astonishing third behind established stars Niki Lauda and Ronnie Peterson.
(Jutta Fausel)

equipment. He had mechanical sympathy. We used to joke with him about his days as a tractor mechanic. He understood what the car was doing, why it was doing it and all the rest of it, so no, he was absolutely not hard on the car at all. Unlike his team-mate at the time, Jean-Pierre Jarier, whose car I was working on. He was completely the opposite. He was fast, but he was completely brutal with the car. Very hard on gearboxes and that side of things. To be fair, Jean-Pierre was fast on his day but was a lot more up and down than Tom. Tom was always on it, every day. No matter what he was in, he was making the car go as fast as it would go.

If I had to pick one stand-out feature of his driving it would be his car control. He had phenomenal car control. That's one of the reasons why he excelled in conditions when the grip levels were low. Whether it was wet, greasy or damp, he was unbelievable. Look at his great win at the Race of Champions at Brands Hatch. Some people would argue that it wasn't a full grid etc… It wasn't who he beat, but the way he did it. When the conditions got a bit iffy, again, his natural talent just came to the fore. The margins looked even bigger. That was what I was trying to get across, that when the conditions got difficult, everybody's pace dropped but Tom's pace dropped far less than anybody else.

Another example would be his second race for us at Dijon. He was super quick, and all the journalists were coming up to us and saying you've just got to go out to the back of the circuit, to the downhill section where all the bends are. He's just amazing to watch! Also, they were clamouring to talk to him about his performance and there's Tom in his almost virgin white overalls. He was completely uncommercialised, sitting in the back of the garage wondering what all the fuss was about. He just didn't understand it. All he was doing was driving a car as fast as he could. It wasn't arrogance at all, it was the pure humility of the guy.

I can think of a few examples which typify the sort of person Tom was. Firstly, Alan Rees going absolutely bonkers at him at one point because apparently – I think it was the guy he used to race with in F3 – had a got a new car or something, and had rung Tom up and asked him if he'd come and test the car and tell him what he thought. Tom just says, "'course I can, no problem." He'd never checked with Alan, and when he found out about it he was not happy at all, and asks him what is he doing? Tom just says, "He's a friend of mine, so I'm helping him out." Off he went and tested the car. Again, the humility of the man.

Secondly, he was very loyal. There was talk in early 1975 that Colin Chapman was trying to swap Ronnie

Peterson for him. Chapman was very keen. I remember talking to Tom about it, and don't forget at that time Lotus was a top team. You know, they were the Mercedes of the day, with much more potential and pedigree than Shadow. Obviously, everybody would have wished him well because he was such a great guy, and we would have been devastated to lose him even though Ronnie was a great driver, but Tom had bonded the team around him so well. I remember Tom saying, "Why would I want to go? I'm happy here!" I'm not saying he wasn't ambitious, that would be disrespectful to him. He was happy in his environment, and that was important to him. In the end, it didn't happen for a whole host of reasons.

Thirdly, how uncommercial he was. At one of the Grands Prix Tom had done a deal with Heuer, the watchmakers, got a free watch and had put one of their badges on his overalls. Again, Alan Rees asks him what he got for the badge? Tom says, "A free watch." Alan says, "Is that all? You're worth far more than that." Tom thought he'd done the deal of the century. Look at me, someone's just given me this very expensive watch and all I've to do is put a badge on my overalls.

He just loved driving cars, absolutely loved it. He just wanted to be in a car every day, all day. That's typified by when he drove the Lancia

Stratos rally car on an event. He loved it, and was super-fast until he crashed. He did have a problem with the lack of headroom in the car, with him being so tall. He told me that he couldn't keep his head straight up because his helmet would catch the roof, so he had to tilt his head over at an angle and drive like that all the time.

When Tom was ever in a car you would always want to watch him on the track. You'd never think of going to sit at the back of the garage and have a cup of tea. You'd always want to be on the pit wall. You'd almost fight to go and hold the pit board out. In that way, you could get on the pit wall and watch him drive. That was what you wanted to do. You'd be doing the pit board and three or four people would be standing there with you because they wanted to watch him as well. Listen to him on the throttle, and his throttle control. His steering inputs you could watch. You *wanted* to watch. You never went back into the garage and thought 'I can't be bothered', and have a cuppa and a biscuit. Every time he went out you just wanted to be on the pit wall, and that's one of the biggest compliments I can pay him.

Everybody wanted to work with Tom, the whole team. He drew the whole team around him. Not one team member had a bad word to say about him. He would speak to everybody when he came to the factory. He would talk to the guys in the machine shop, the fabrication shop etc... We're not talking about the size of the teams these days. He was just a normal guy. His background helped, for sure. You knew he'd had a good upbringing. His dad was such a nice guy, always grateful to the team. Thanked all the mechanics when he came to the races. Just a great family atmosphere.

A small mention of Nella because she was phenomenal as well. Everyone in the team loved her. In some ways they were an unlikely couple, with her coming from a different background, while in others they weren't. She was always very glamorous and presentable, and obviously gorgeous in lots of ways, but she would also speak to everybody in a nice way. I've experienced in the past that many haven't been like that. Because you are seen as a non-crucial part of it you don't need to be spoken to. Nella was just as friendly and as nice as Tom was.

It was such a tragedy what happened to him. I'd left Shadow by then and had gone to work for Tyrrell, so I was at the Grand Prix. I remember to this day, vividly, being on the pit wall because I was still a number two mechanic hanging out the pit signalling board. I remember it happening. I wouldn't say it happened in front of me, but it was

You never tire of seeing images like this. This one – although it could be any of the circuits Tom graced with his otherworldly car control – is Zandvoort in 1975. **(Rob Petersen)**

about 100 yards further down the track. I mean, we knew he'd hit the marshal but his car had gone over the brow and out of sight down the straight. We noticed he didn't come around and assumed that the car had been damaged and he'd parked it. You could never have dreamt what had happened and it was only when the race had finished that somebody asked if I'd heard about Tom, and then the full story came out. Back then, the race continued and nobody had said anything.

There just seemed a darkness over the whole paddock. Nobody smiled. Normally after a race, you're relieved to be packing up whether you've done well or had a bad day. If you'd done well you'd have a smile on your face. I didn't see anybody with a smile on their face at all. Nobody, and I mean nobody. It was such a tragedy. In that era you never got used to it, but you sort of expected it. You were surprised, upset at the time, but you were never shocked. It happened too often for you to be shocked.

I think it's important that Tom should be remembered, and that people should know about him. It just brings it back to you when you relive it in such detail that you almost put yourself back there, don't you? I've got a tear in my eye now. I'm sorry, it shouldn't have that effect, should it? He certainly left an impression on me. Tom had everything in him to win numerous Grands Prix, and ultimately have a crack at the world championship. No doubt, no doubt at all.

DEBBIE JONES
Family Friend

My Mum, Anne, was a nurse with 'Aunty' Gwyn, and lived with them for a while before she married my dad, Alun. She said that, when he was a little boy, she used to take Maldwyn on days out when his parents were working. Getting ready for bedtime she had a heck of a struggle getting him scrubbed down and washing his hair, as he would grumble non-stop. They'd go and stay at a caravan in Plas Coch, Menai Straits, and he'd enjoy winging things at her as they walked along the river. She described him as a little monkey, always active and full of mischief.

Much later on, when he was well into his racing career, Maldwyn had broken his leg after an incident in the Monaco F3 race, and was struggling to get into his 'plane seat when a young chap stepped in to help and make him comfy. It turned out to be Mick Jagger. Maldwyn's comment on returning home was, "Mam, he was very nice, but I think he forgot to wash that morning!"

Dad was in touch with Eddie Knipe, the huge fan from South Africa, at the time of organising the Ruthin memorial, and sent him the exhaust pipe and a box of Champion sparkplugs from the Formula Ford Maldwyn won via the *Daily Express* newspaper after claiming the championship. Dad still has the oil can and pistons that Mald used on that car.

Alan Henry, the journalist, was extremely fond of Maldwyn, as he was a common lad with no monied background who managed to do so well for himself. He spoke at a memorial service in Ruthin after the funeral.

Warm, crinkly eyes and an easy smile – that's how I remember Mald. At the age of around seven I was probably his youngest fan. I was always disappointed when Mum and Dad went off with Aunty Gwyn and 'Uncle' Jack to watch him race at Silverstone or Brands Hatch, and had to content myself with the UOP Shadow stickers etc... they brought back. I only got to Silverstone myself a couple of years after his tragic accident. I met James Hunt and Niki Lauda, and was mad about the mini-motorbikes they used to bomb about in the pits. I just knew that if he had still been alive Mald would have got me a ride on one of them!

He was something of a superhero to me. I was in awe of him, always jetting off to some other part of the world for a race. He made a fuss of me and made me feel special, so I was none too pleased when he returned home to Braeburn (a bungalow where Jack and Gwyn lived) one time in his blue MG, with a lady friend in tow. Apparently, I had a face like thunder as I looked her up and down in her checked blouse and blue dungarees. How I sneered at her stripy socks... Nella.

As we all sat down with tea and cake Aunty Gwyn announced that she and I would sing along to the new single from Queen, *Bohemian Rhapsody*, still a favourite song of mine. So I sang my little heart out for him, and when the song ended he was beaming. Everyone was beaming, and I turned smugly to my right where she sat. How clever I was, Nella said, remembering all those words when she couldn't manage it, and what a lovely singing voice I had. I couldn't help but warm to her after that.

I only wish Aunty Gwyn and Uncle Jack were here to see this, as I still miss them terribly.

Wouldn't it be wonderful if Maldwyn could know how fondly he is remembered?

UOP Shadow promo card. **(Alun Jones)**

Debbie, when she was seven years old, prepares to say goodbye to Tom before he sets off on his globe-trotting adventures. **(Alun Jones)**

ALUN JONES
Family Friend

My wife Anne had been a friend of Gwyn's for a number of years before I met her in 1965, and a few months after we started courting I was taken to meet Jack and Gwyn, becoming a close friend myself in a relatively short time.

The photo opposite shows Anne and me sitting with Gwyn outside the UOP hospitality unit at the British Grand Prix at Silverstone in 1975.

Jack must have been tempted inside to sample the fabulous food laid on by our hosts. Representatives from UOP were quite happy to chat with us about Tom and life in general.

Later on that Friday evening, after all the day's action had concluded, we all went along with personnel from the other teams to a pre-race dinner at one of the big hotels in Northampton. I remember that all the drivers were told to go to bed at around 9pm. When I think back to that dinner, the only person present who's still involved in Formula One today is Frank Williams.

When the race had been stopped early due to the atrocious weather we headed back to Jack and Gwyn's caravan, which was located in the nearest field to the track. By the time we got there, the weather had deteriorated even further and the whole field was awash. Needless to say, the entertainment for the rest of the evening was watching cars getting bogged down as they were trying to leave, while other people were diving into their tents or caravans. One section of the field was on two levels, so those on the bottom level had no chance, even with about a dozen people trying to push them!

A piston from Tom's Formula Ford and an oil can used by Tom during that period. Both prized possessions of Alun's. **(Alun Jones)**

Fortunately for us, we weren't leaving until the following morning (Sunday).

A couple of months before the Grand Prix we had been invited to Tom and Nella's wedding, in Otford, Kent. We picked Jack and Gwyn up and all travelled down together. Nella's family had booked a hotel for us to stay in.

We went the following year to Brands Hatch for the Grand Prix, but no hospitality this time – UOP was no longer involved – which meant we (Anne and myself) had to pay. We went to the pits with Jack and Gwyn on Saturday, to see Tom. Then on race day (Sunday), the four of us stayed put throughout the morning at Paddock Hill Bend, having got up very early to claim a good viewing position.

Talking of Brands Hatch, the boss of the circuit, John Webb, called Jack a couple of months after Tom's passing and invited him down to reminisce about the time Tom garaged his Lola Formula Ford at the circuit, long before his progression to Formula One. He even took us

---

Mr & Mrs M. H. Warwick-Smith

request the pleasure of

the company of

Mr & Mrs R. A. Jones

at the marriage of their daughter

Nella

with

Mr Thomas Maldwyn Pryce

at St. Bartholomew's Church, Otford,

on Saturday, April 5th 1975

at 3.30 p.m.

Reception afterwards at

Donnington Manor, Danton Green.

Shorehill Farm,
Otford Hills,
Sevenoaks, Kent.

R.S.V.P.
Black Tie

The invitation to Tom and Nella's wedding. **(Alun Jones)**

around the track at some pace in a Ford Escort Mk2.

As a family (Anne and our young daughter Debbie and me), we still went to the 1977 British Grand Prix and we were able to use the pit passes given to us by Jack and Gwyn, who understandably weren't up to attending. We arrived back in Ruthin with the large framed photo of Tom at the Nurburgring taken the year before, which had been put together by all the Shadow mechanics who had an inscription put on the frame that read: 'From all Tom's Friends at Shadow Cars.' I do remember we had a heck of a job fitting the photo in our little Hillman Imp, with the three of us and our camping gear.

A somewhat different event was when Tom was competing in the Tour of Epynt rally in the Lancia Stratos, in 1975. Jack was driving Tom's MGB – Tom had been given a top of the range Opel as part of their advertising campaign, so I believe – and I can testify that Jack was a safe and fast driver himself. Much later on when he was in his late seventies, he was still the same. I base this on the fact that I loved speed myself, my first love being motorbikes. A BSA Gold Star and a Triumph Bonneville being the order of the day. Plus, there were no speed cameras back then. Happy days.

I have a few mementoes from Tom's career, such as an oil jug –

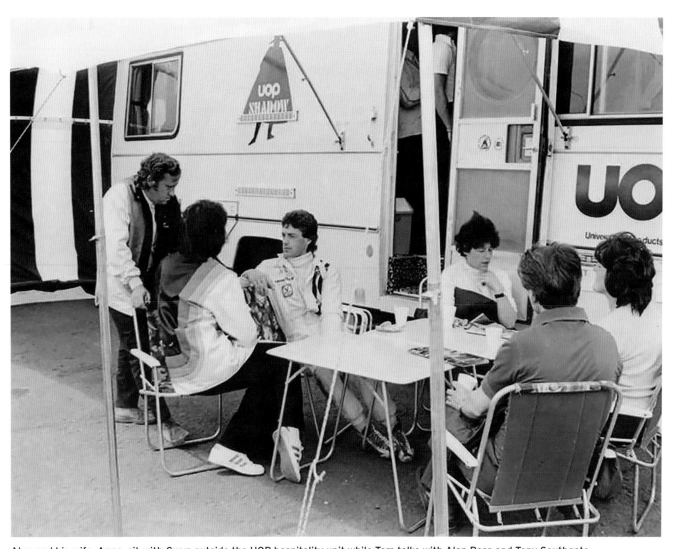

Alun and his wife, Anne, sit with Gwyn outside the UOP hospitality unit while Tom talks with Alan Ress and Tony Southgate. **(Dave Jones Collection)**

which I still use to this day – and a piston from his Lola FF1600. When Eddie Knipe – the huge fan of Tom's from South Africa – was organising the memorial in Ruthin, I sent him the exhaust pipe and a box of Champion spark plugs, again from the Lola.

To this day I still think that if Tom had taken up Colin Chapman's offer to drive a Lotus in 1977, things would have turned out so much different. But Tom was loyal to the Shadow team that gave him his first works drive in Formula One.

IAN FLUX

Token Mechanic/Racing Driver

I was an apprentice mechanic in a BMC garage. I got slung out of college and, because of that, the owner wouldn't have me back in the place. I was already racing karts then, and the owner knew I was interested in racing. He knew of a vacancy at Token, where they were looking for someone to sweep the floors, make tea and drive the van. He said I could go there on a two-week trial and, if I fucked up, that would be it, but if I cracked on with things they would keep me.

I was at Token three days and it was like a lightbulb moment. I thought, "Fucking hell, I love this!" and that was it. There were four others in the team. Ray Jessop, Neil Trundle, Chris Lewis and Tom, of course.

I first met him when he came for a seat fitting. I'd seen him race at Brands in '73, so I knew who he was. He didn't have a fucking clue who I was! The next time I saw him was when we were hoping to test at Goodwood prior to the International Trophy at Silverstone. Tom had lost his road licence, so somebody dropped him off. I was doing Formula Vee in 1974 and I had a Volkswagen caravanette that me and my dad used to sleep in when we went racing. We

did one all-nighter and the next until about three in the morning. Tom slept in my caravanette. He couldn't drive anywhere because he didn't have that license!

Tom was a fantastic driver. The older you get the more you look back, and I've been in racing for 46 years now. The more you realise he was totally gifted. Racing drivers are quite simple. You can either do it or you can't.

I did all the F1 races with Token, but I didn't go to Monaco for the F3 race. I helped with preparing the car but they didn't need me there. Afterwards we went to Goodwood to test, which I think was on the following Thursday. We started running about 10am, and about 11ish Hesketh arrived in their helicopter. Then, within minutes, Shadow arrived in their helicopter! I can remember Tom saying, "Look, I think I'm gonna have to go and sort out a drive, boys." We knew we had no money. All everybody was for – Neil Trundle especially – was for Tom to get a decent drive. So Tom went to see both teams and came back after lunch. We were all sitting around and he came over and said, "Right, good news boys. I've got myself a good job, got

A young Ian Flux (bottom right) works on Tom's Token, while the ever-flamboyant Chris Meek smiles for the camera. **(James Beckett Collection)**

some wages and I've joined Shadow." We were all made up for him. There was no sadness because we knew that we couldn't offer him anything. Everybody was just really happy that he got what he deserved and was going to a decent team.

In 1976 I'd moved up to F3 and I was testing at Snetterton on a Thursday afternoon. In those days testing was for anybody. Ronnie Peterson was there, who was my hero, and Tom. I was sharing the track with them. Tom would go past

and Peterson would go past and I thought, "Fucking hell, here's me on the same track with one guy I know and one I'd like to know." You're not going to be testing an F3 car these days and Lewis Hamilton goes past.

I followed his career. After Token, Neil Trundle got me a job with Graham Hill's team. Even when I was there it was "Where's Tom on the grid?" more than where are we on the grid! I can remember the day he died. I was doing a F3 race at Silverstone, where I was

Tom made his Formula One debut in the Token at the non-championship International Trophy, held at Silverstone on April 7th, 1974. He is seen here leading Tom Belso's Formula 5000 Lola and John Nicholson's Lyncar. **(Jeff Bloxham)**

standing chatting with Ian Taylor after we'd just finished practice. I can remember Ian Titchmarsh coming on the speaker and saying he had very, very sad news from South Africa. Unfortunately, a couple of hours ago

Tom Pryce was killed at the circuit and that there were no further details at the moment.

I didn't like funerals because, when Graham Hill's plane went down I went to six funerals in five days. I was

only 19 at the time and, looking back, it really did my head in. I wanted to remember Tom how I last saw him. In 2014 Karl Jones took me to his grave.

Tom was very naturally gifted as a driver. I was just the gopher in the

team but he looked at me as his equal. He never saw himself as the racing driver and me as just the van driver. He spoke to me as an equal person, and that's probably why I liked him so much.

EDDIE KNIPE

Fan

Thomas Maldwyn Pryce was a name which meant little or nothing to me before 1974. This well respected, unassuming young gentleman of the Formula One circuit had sparked my imagination only when all things Welsh began to grab my attention, this especially due to the all-conquering successes of the Welsh rugby teams of the Seventies. Tom Pryce may well have been mentioned in the same breath with fellow countrymen such as Gareth Edwards, Phil Bennett, JPR Williams, JJ Williams and Mervyn Davies, but sadly, this was not to be.

I had treacherously forsaken my allegiance to the mighty Springbok rugby team of that era and started supporting all teams of a British flavour. It was not that I had completely alienated myself from my country's national team, but I used to feel sorry for the touring teams who travelled to our shores and were so far away from their homes and families. Well, that was my reasoning and I was much younger then.

Tom became my sporting hero after I read an article about him in a copy of *Autosport* magazine and saw pictures of him in the famous 'green'

magazine, *Motor Sport*. The fact that he wore a white helmet with five black stripes emblazoned on the front further intrigued me and stirred my interest.

I was at college when he met his untimely death and was playing in a cricket match that afternoon. I was listening to the Grand Prix at Kyalami on a small transistor radio, waiting on my turn to go out and bat. Brief news of the accident was described by the commentator, but no further details were announced. It was only after I had returned to the side of the field after my rather short stint at the crease that the awful events which had transpired at Kyalami became evident. I had lost my two favourite cousins, Barry and Peter, the previous year, in what was a totally unnecessary accident. Now, in another unfortunate incident, my favourite Formula One driver had lost his life.

Many years later, in 2002, I would take up a teaching post in Sevenoaks, just a few miles from Otford. In 2007 I stumbled upon the resting place of one Thomas Maldwyn Pryce in St Bartholomew's graveyard. It was then that I wrote to Ruthin town council and hoped to persuade them to look

into having Tom honoured in his home region.

A forum that I started on the *Autosport* website raised much awareness around the world, and it was heart-warming to realise that so many people still remembered Tom Pryce and they were genuinely interested in the progress made by the memorial trust. Some were even making plans to attend the unveiling of the memorial wall in Upper Clwyd Street in Ruthin.

After two years of perseverance, and much deliberation about how to fund the project, the memorial trust – of which I had become a proud member – gained a major financial boost through the generous assistance of all the 2009 Formula One teams. Bernie Ecclestone secured two pit passes for all of the European Grands Prix that season. Through a Tom Pryce memorial website fans could bid for these passes. A substantial amount of money was raised, which enabled us to have the memorial unveiled in Ruthin on June 11th, 2009, what would have been Tom's 60th birthday.

Nella Pryce was afforded the honour of removing the Welsh flag to reveal the bronze plaque, a proud moment for her and Tom's mother,

Gwyneth. Sadly, Tom's father Jack had passed away whilst preparations were being made to honour Tom in Ruthin. My thoughts were not only with Thomas Maldwyn Pryce's family and friends on the June 11th, 2009, but also with another family a good few thousand miles away in South Africa.

Eddie Knipe was instrumental in the campaign to have Tom honoured in his homeland. His vision was realised in 2009 when Nella Pryce unveiled the striking memorial to her late husband, watched by David Richards. **(Mark Welch)**

JACKIE OLIVER

Racing Driver and Shadow Team Administrator

I was living in the United States in the seventies, and coming back to Europe to drive for JW Porsche and Alan Mann. I had houses in both places, so was hopping the pond the whole time. The main reason for that was Shadow and UOP (United Oil Products) was in the USA. We decided to make the Formula One cars in the UK, instead of in the United States. I ended up moving to Chicago – where UOP was based – with Don. I ran both organisations and still raced as and when I wanted to. The Seventies is all a bit of a blur. Life was so hectic then.

Alan (Rees) spoke to me about Tom after his Formula 3 win at Monaco in '74 and asked me what I thought. I said he was good because all the best drivers are quick at Monte Carlo. To be fast around there you've got to have a lot of smooth control. You can be fast, but you can hit the barrier very easily.

Tom was one of those guys who had a talent that came from nowhere. Where his speed came from was being so relaxed in the car, never fighting it. I don't think he was very good at sorting cars out, because he was so relaxed and would drive by the seat of his pants. He would drive around any

problems with the car rather than try to make the car quicker. He tended to drive a bit sideways the whole time. He liked a loose rear end. The cars then, you could get away with it. You couldn't now.

I was running the CanAm team, and then when that stopped in 1974 we put a Formula 5000 car together. Don always wanted to run two-car teams in the States, which was no problem, but we had to get a driver who was going to get the job done. The Formula One program was soaking up most of the budget. The best person to talk to about drivers was Alan. Then I used to call them up, or Don would talk to them directly when he got into the swing of it, and hire the drivers, with Alan running the program.

I think Don wanted to see whether someone was going to be quicker (in the F5000) than me. I said fine, but the difficulty you're going to have is that all these drivers are pretty good, but it takes a little bit of time to get used to the car. Just bunging someone in against someone like me, then they're at a disadvantage. The Dodge engine we used had more power than the Chevy but weighed an extra 50kg. Tony Southgate used it in

a Formula One chassis, and I don't think Tom was very happy with it at Long Beach in '75.

When it came to whether we kept drivers or got rid of them, Don and I would sit down and talk about it. The F1 swap deal with Tom and Ronnie (Peterson) was a deal we couldn't do in the end. I think it was to do with money.

I used to get so upset when the F1 car would suffer from stupid faults and cause Tom to retire from races on a number of occasions. Half the time the car was midfield or better, but we weren't finishing the bloody races.

The CEO of UOP told me that they were going to be taken over by Signal Oil in '76, and it could cause problems with the sponsorship. At the end of '75, the UOP sponsorship ceased, so I came back to Europe to try and find some money for the Formula One team but was still driving the F5000 car in the States. I found a guy called Franco Ambrosio, who wanted Renzo Zorzi in the car.

I went to Kyalami to liaise with Franco because I was the only one who could speak Italian. He was great fun, but a complete bloody lunatic. Alan wasn't happy with

Franco's choice of driver, Zorzi. I offered to talk to him over a Campari and soda, to see whether we could get rid of Zorzi. Alan was very happy with Tom, and Tom was a good gauge for how slow Renzo was!

I didn't see Tom's accident, but I spoke to Laffite afterwards and asked him what happened. He said, "Tom came flying past me, didn't bother to put the brakes on, and took me out at the first corner." I said, "Because he was already dead." The most bizarre accident.

It was the first time I'd got involved in sorting out the problems after a fatality, and I had to go the mortuary. I looked at Tom, and I didn't recognise him. A horrendous accident, what a shame. I had to get his body back to the UK and talk with Nella. That was the end of it for me. I would do one more year of driving and then stop. It was unfortunate, because he was getting better.

After Tom's death Don asked, "What are we gonna do now?" At least we had Riccardo Patrese, and had got rid of Zorzi, but now we needed another driver. I flew back and talked with Alan in my house in London. Then we took the FIA

Very much on the limit through Paddock Hill Bend in the Shadow DN3. British Grand Prix, 1974. **(Paul Kooyman)**

Yearbook out of the bookcase, which had a list of all the graded drivers in it. When I got to J, I said, "Alan Jones." He'd fallen out with Surtees. Jonesy had told me he'd had enough of it and was going back to Australia. So, I got a number and called him up in Australia. I said, "Hello mate, do you want to drive for Shadow?" He accepted, but couldn't get there until a certain date, so I drove in the Race of Champions. Then Riccardo had a clash of dates later on, and I also drove the Shadow in the Swedish Grand Prix. What a shame, because we would have had Riccardo and Tom, or Jonesy and Tom. How strange the world is. It was a dangerous business then. The cars were fragile.

I started my Formula One career when Jimmy Clark got killed, and it was a terrible baptism of fire. In my first Formula One race, I replaced probably the best driver in the world, and Colin's best friend. It was a nightmare. In the end I didn't stay at Lotus because it was such a difficult first year.

When it came to team-mates or drivers who were driving cars I had an interest in, you would try and remove yourself from the personality of the person. It's a protection mechanism. Tom would have ended up at Arrows I suppose, if he'd still been driving for Shadow. A case of what might have been.

Formula One is larger than life. The bizarre accident that killed Tom, you couldn't make it up. Astonishing. He was just a very nice guy. Socially he was great, with Nella. I remember that, very fondly.

JORGE KOECHLIN

Racing Driver/Friend

I wanted to be a race car driver all my life. My father was a pilot in Peru, and he tried to help me. I went through the Bob Bondurant racing school by selling Peruvian handcrafts in 1971. I had been reading *Road & Track* magazine in Peru, and Rob Walker was always mentioning Brands Hatch in his articles. Brands Hatch this, Brands Hatch that... I had been to Indianapolis, and through friends, I met Tony Hulman. Then I went to England. My sister worked for Pan Am at the time, so she was able to get me a one-way ticket. Peru was under a communist military dictatorship, so I went off and I stayed in a bed and breakfast in London. I asked the landlord where Brands Hatch was, but he didn't know and nor did anyone else I asked. Obviously, my accent didn't help! Finally, I heard a knock on the door of my room. It was the landlord and he was so happy. He said, "I've found where you wish to go. It's on the A20. This is what you have to do. You have to go to Hyde Park Corner, and there is a green bus, number 19. That is gonna take you to Brands Hatch."

Off I went and when I got there, I asked at Brands where I could stay.

They said, "Across the road, there's a mad woman. You can go and stay there. We have nothing to do with it!" So I went there and a lady named Red opened the door and said, "Who are you, what do you want?" Then she said something I'll never forget. She told me I could stay for seven pounds a week with food included, and that I would be sharing with a Yank. With my limited English then I thought I was being put in the stables with a yak! Anyway, I said okay. I didn't have the money for anything else, only about 300 dollars in my pocket.

I went into a room and there were two small beds, and there was a skinny fellow who said hello and asked me my name. I said "Jorge". "What?" I said again "Jorge". He asked where I came from, so I told him Peru, and that I spoke Spanish. "Ah, okay. We'll name you 'Pancho.'" So that became my nickname at Red's, and the Yank was Danny Sullivan.

Some time later a Ford Cortina drove up to the house, and out came a lanky fellow with Wellington boots. I may exaggerate, but he probably still had cow shit on them! He also didn't know how to speak proper English, and that was Maldwyn. But we all called him Thomas.

I got a job working at Eldens and bought a Merlyn Mk20A that had been advertised in *Autosport* for a few weeks. It belonged to a very promising Canadian driver called David Loring. He was selling it with four huge chests full of spares, and I bought a transporter for it which had a bed and an oven in it. Eldens paid me ten pounds a week, putting cars together. Seven pounds of that went to Red, and I was left with three pounds. With Thomas, I would drive to Sevenoaks station on Wednesday nights. I would go on the train from there to Victoria station, about seven or eight at night. There was a news stand in Victoria station where you could get *Motoring News* and *Autosport*, which were due out on a Thursday. I would read *Motoring News* on the way back to Sevenoaks, where Thomas would be waiting for me rain or shine. I would jump in the car, hand him the *Motoring News*, and I would start reading *Autosport*. We would both sit there, underneath a light, and read the comics. Then we would go back to Red's house and first thing in the morning we would continue to read them.

A lot of the time the two of us would go to the tracks. Wednesday

was Brands, Silverstone was open on Tuesdays I think, Snetterton on Thursdays, and then if there was no bike meeting, Brands was open on Saturdays. We would go together and share the petrol. We'd just hang around and talk to people like Bob Marston of Lola, the man with the pipe. Eric (Broadley) would show up sometimes and take off the nosecone of whatever car they were testing. Then he would jump on the front of the monocoque and look at the shock absorbers. That was the way he checked the settings! We'd go to Snetterton and Jim Russell would be there with his son-in-law, Ralph Firman. That's where I met Roberto Guerrero for the first time.

At Red's house, we would sit in the bay window looking at the garden with the pond and the gnomes, and traffic going by on the A20. We would drive Lassie (Red's dog) crazy by tapping on the windowsill, and Red would come and get mad at us. I still have the picture in my head. There were two sofas, a chair for George (Red's husband), and two chairs looking out of the window. Thomas absolutely adored Martin, their son. He would play with him and look after him.

We were very good friends. Thomas would come and help with the Merlyn. Of course, we were both useless and hopeless. I once tried to get him in the car to see what he thought it was like, but we both decided we weren't 'set-up' drivers and it wasn't worth the risk of crashing the Merlyn.

Thomas would always drink shandy. We would go to a pub called The Mill, somewhere around Otford. There were two girls there, one red-haired and the other black-haired. I met these two girls and brought them over, and Thomas was very shy. It was Nella and her sister, Penny. I went out with Penny and Thomas went out with Nella.

We would wake up in the morning at Red's and listen to the engines being warmed up at Brands. We could recognise whether it was a Matra, a Ferrari or a Cossie. All the gatekeepers at Brands were our friends and we would go there every day. There was a lovely landlady at the bar called Angie. Once I walked in and Paul Newman was there getting drinks out of a vending machine. Red would always go on about 'Clarkie' (Geoff Clarke) and Tony (Lanfranchi), saying all they did was get pissed at that pub.

At Brands, there was an entrance gate near Dingle Dell that we knew was always open. One night we took two girls around the circuit about 11

Tom joining in the fun with Nella to his right and Penny, Nella's sister, on his left. It was Jorge who approached both Nella and Penny when out with Tom, that led to Tom and Nella becoming an item. Nella remembers: "This is one of my family's photos taken way back before Thomas and I got married. It's taken at my parent's house before we were probably going out to a fancy dress party or something. We had a big trunk of 'dressing up clothes' since we were children, that we had fun with when going to parties." **(Nella Pryce)**

o'clock at night, with no lights, flat out! They were screaming their heads off. I was in the back seat with one. With Thomas being shy about who he was and, later on, he said, "We should not have done that. That was not the proper thing to do. What were we thinking?"

I remember going with him to Maurice Gomm's place for his seat fitting when he got the Rondel drive. Thomas raced at Rouen with them, and I asked him how it was when he came back. He said, "I came into the pits and they asked what I wanted." He never knew what he wanted. For example, 'Master' James (Hunt) would always say, "Give me more castor." He had some fixation with castor. Anyway, Thomas said, "I tried to look clever and asked them to drop the wing a little bit. I didn't know what to ask for, but I had to ask for something to make them think I knew about cars!" When he came back in they were all jumping up and down with the lap time he'd done. He also came back with a beautiful Gitanes T-shirt, and I was really envious of it. He was very happy, wearing that T-shirt everywhere.

Thomas was up there as a driver. We both thought Jim Clark was the best, but he wasn't that style of driver. He was a natural talent like Ronnie (Peterson), but Thomas was a better race car driver. The Royale RP11 Thomas drove was such a lousy

Jorge remembers Tom wringing the neck of the sometimes recalcitrant Royale Formula Three car on many occasions.
(Chris Walker/Kartpix/Maureen Magee)

car. He used to wrestle that thing through Clearways on opposite lock. It was such a bad car, but it actually made his name. He could make it go where nobody else could make it work.

In 2005 or 2006 I went to England and then drove along the coast of Wales on the B-roads to get to Ruthin. I stopped at a square and there was some sort of government

office. I went in and told the lady I was looking for Mr Jack Pryce. She knew exactly who I meant, and asked what I was doing there. I explained that I was a friend of his son, and the lady was really touched. She asked me where I'd come from. We were almost in tears, the two of us. She told me where he lived, and I made my way there, but got lost and stopped the post lady who pointed out the

house. Jack didn't know I was coming. I stayed there for a long while, and Jack told me Thomas liked me very much and would always talk about 'Pancho.' He also told me, as a young boy, Thomas would design cars in his notebooks. We had a long, long chat in his conservatory. I'm lucky to be alive. I think that Thomas and Stefan Bellof were the two great talents that we lost.

NICK JORDAN

Mechanic

Preparing for the start of the Monaco Formula Three race, Nick Jordan (in the blue shirt, with tool tray) is on patrol looking for anything untoward. **(James Beckett Collection)**

My abiding memory of Tom concerns the Monaco F3 in 1974. I was mechanic to Tony Brise that day and we were sitting on the grid behind Tom, who had qualified on pole position, when I noticed that Neil Trundle, who was looking after Tom, had a slave battery by the car to help start the engine. We were both using Pinto engines, which were damn heavy and they were a fucking bitch to start. An absolute bitch! The Bendix type starter was just not up to the job.

To overcome the problem I had made a bracket up and put a 6v motorcycle battery on the car to supplement the 12v battery, giving it 18v at the starter, which gave it a boost. I knew we wouldn't have a problem because we'd tested it beforehand.

Anyway, I walked across to Neil and said, "Look Neil, you can't use a slave battery because in the regulations it says that the car has got to start under its own merit." I knew all this because I'd read the rule book. Neil looks at me and I think his words were something like "You bastard." Don't get me wrong, Neil's a lovely guy, but I said, "I'm sorry,

Neil, but I just had to tell you." I didn't protest him or anything, I just pointed it out.

It didn't matter in the end, because Tom was right on it. He had a better car than what Tony had on that day. The total package was there, and Tom was a super-quick driver. I take my hat off to him for his performance. He

was just a very, very good driver. We saw what he did in Formula One, and then, sadly, you know his demise was very, very sad.

I never knew him as a friend, personally. More of a nodding acquaintance, to say hello to in the paddock. He was a very shy bloke. He had a gritty determination and

great car control. I remember Roger (Williamson) – another driver I worked with – saying, "That kid's good." The Royale he drove in F3 wasn't the best car. It was unfancied. I've earned a living in motorsport for nearly fifty years now and I've never heard anyone say a bad word about Tom. Never, and I mean that sincerely.

BOB HEWITT

Freelance Photojournalist and Acquaintance

My first contact with Maldwyn was when I arranged a feature on him for the *Liverpool Daily Post*. It was written by a reporter, John Griffiths. I took all the photos for the piece. At that time I was also going to races at Oulton Park, Mallory Park etc... and providing photographs for some newspapers, but mainly for *Autosport* and *Motoring News*. I had first noticed his name, and that he came from North Wales like myself, at a club meeting at Oulton Park when he was racing in FF1600 in the early seventies. From then onwards I followed his career, with him being local to me.

Eventually, we got to be quite friendly and my wife and I would go and visit him at his mum and dad's. Jack and Gwyn were lovely people. If I had to cover one of the race meetings and Maldwyn was racing, I'd take Jack along with me. We did that on a number of occasions. At the time I had a Lotus Cortina Mk1, and I was always worried about whether I was speeding with Jack being the police sergeant in Ruthin. He always said he didn't mind.

My wife and I were once invited up to their beautiful house up in the Clocaenog forest. It was Maldwyn who had got in touch to say they were having a celebratory party one evening after he had won the 100 bottles of Champagne at Brands Hatch. He gave us one of the bottles. I've never particularly enjoyed Champagne, but I wish to this day that I'd kept it as a memento. You just don't think at the time. Sadly, that was the last time I saw Maldwyn alive.

After the birth of our daughter I got a bit sensible in the mid-seventies and sold the Lotus Cortina, and I bought a grey Rover 2000. Imagine, going from one of the most exciting cars to the most mundane thing you would ever wish to drive. It was in the said Rover that I heard the tragic news. I'd been asked to cover a Sheffield Wednesday match that day, and was on my way up and over the tops towards Sheffield with a couple of local lads who were twins, David and Alan Williams. They were from Sheffield originally, and jumped at the chance of a lift.

It must have been coming up to one o'clock when I switched the radio on and heard the news of what had happened. I just had to stop the car in the first lay-by and got out and left them there. They must have been thinking, 'what's up with him?' They had no idea. It was just abject shock at the tragedy. Sadly, at that time in motor racing, you know, people did get killed frequently. The whole thing, the marshal running across the track, the extinguisher, the whole thing. Absolutely dreadful. I must admit, I don't think I went to a race meeting after that for quite a while. Even if I was offered an assignment I'd say "No thanks." I find it hard, even today, to look at the negatives from that era.

At that time there weren't many people from the North Wales area achieving any sort of recognition. Not just in sport, but anything. There was a pride in that it was someone from North Wales that was achieving something. There was so much hope, so much hope. He was on the brink. Whether he would have achieved any real success with Shadow or anyone else, who knows. He just had something a bit special. The world was lighting up for him, when...

His achievements were based on his ability and his passion. That's another great sadness, that his potential was never realised to the full extent. I am sure they saw it in his early days at Royale, thinking he was a guy going places. Every car he got in, he was quick immediately. I suppose he was very much like Jim Clark in that respect. Never mind being in the garage changing this and that. He would just jump in any car and drive it, quickly. Some people just have that gift. It comes naturally and they enhance that ability in any way they can.

I still watch every Grand Prix, which is something I've been doing since 1970, but there's always a tinge of sadness because of what happened to Maldwyn. There's always that feeling of what might have been?

After the accident I kept in touch a little bit with Jack and Gwyn. To my shame, not as much as I should have done. I wrote to them after a respectful time, but how long is a respectful time? I found it easier that way. It was very difficult. You feel so awkward and helpless. My trouble would have been that every time I would have seen them, I would have broken down. I know it destroyed the pair of them. How can you even comprehend losing a child? Forget about him being a racing driver. He was their son.

Bob saw some of Tom's early races at Oulton Park. On this occasion it is a BOC Championship round in March 1971, Tom leads Bernard Vermilio and Stan Matthews. **(Bob Hewitt)**

Maldwyn was absolutely down to earth. No airs and graces. Take the time he invited us to help him celebrate with the 100 bottles of Champagne. There was no need for him to get in touch with me and ask us both to come up. It was the kind of gracious person he was. He never forgot his roots or his friends. Let's face it, that's not so easy to do when you are based so far away at Brands Hatch. He was just a great chap.

ENID TOFT

Widow of Colin Toft (Maldwyn's Childhood Friend)

I met Colin in 1971, so I only knew Maldwyn from then. All the lads, and us girls, would all traipse over to Oulton Park to watch him race. Colin would go much further afield, but I never did. We always watched in the same place, so that Maldwyn would know we were there. It was down the bottom of the circuit, Cascades I think it was. We knew the number of his car, so every time he went past we would all cheer. We'd always go and see him before and after his race. If it was raining we'd wrap ourselves in a polythene sheet. We were the driest there. It's fabled about Maldwyn and his driving in the wet. He was absolutely brilliant in the wet.

We got married in August '73 and Maldwyn flew back, especially, from Sweden where he was racing in Formula Two to be at our wedding. I have a photo of Maldwyn at our wedding with my sisters, who were my bridesmaids. My younger sister, Carys, had pictures of Maldwyn on her bedroom wall. She thought he was gorgeous. He was a good-looking lad, wasn't he? Whenever one of the gang – Trefor Williams, Brian Holland – got married Maldwyn would always make sure he was there.

We all went down to his wedding in Kent. We had a Ford Cortina at the time, and there were six of us in it. Colin drove all the way until the outskirts of London, and then Brian took over because Colin didn't know his way through London. Brian had been to Brands Hatch with Maldwyn, so knew where to go. It was lovely. Maldwyn wanted some Welsh harp music played at the wedding, so my auntie – who knew Jack and Gwyneth and was well-known locally – came down with her husband and played at the service. He got married on 5th April 1975, and the service didn't start until five o'clock, so before it we were all watching the Grand National on the television. I can see Maldwyn now in his brown velvet suit, sitting there with his legs up on the coffee table because he didn't want to crease his trousers. Funny, after all this time, you remember such silly things.

He never forgot his friends and would come and see us and the rest of the gang when he came home to see his Mum and Dad. I remember him calling to see us and saying to Colin that he'd met this gorgeous girl. This wasn't long after he'd met Nella. When they all got together they all spoke Welsh. Colin always used to tease him about his posh English accent. He did sound ever so posh. When he gave interviews he didn't sound like the Maldwyn we knew.

After he'd won the Race of Champions he had this massive party at his mum and dad's house just outside Clocaenog. We were all there, the old gang. He brought a couple of crates of the champagne that he'd won and we all got a bottle each. It was a night and a half.

Colin used to talk about Maldwyn a great deal. They'd known each other from when they went to school in Nantglyn when they were five or six-years-old. He would collect anything he could find on his achievements, newspaper cuttings etc...

We were all devastated when he had his accident. I don't think I'd ever seen Colin cry so much. It was horrendous. I'd heard about it on the radio. It was dreadful, just dreadful. Colin was working that day and I was trying to get hold of him on the phone. When I got in touch with him he hadn't heard. He couldn't believe it. I didn't go to the funeral. None of the girls went, but all the lads went. Colin went with Trefor (Williams), Brian (Holland) and Ellis (Wyn Jones), and they took the parish minister from Ruthin, Mr

The old group are reunited again. Tom never forgot his roots or his childhood friends. **(Enid Toft)**

Parry, with them. He was very friendly with Jack and Gwyneth and wanted to be there, but didn't fancy the drive down. Colin did say you didn't have to watch your Ps and Qs with him, he was so 'with it'.

I got quite a surprise a few years ago when I was out walking not far from where I live now. I was approaching the house of Peter Williams, who went to school with Colin and Maldwyn, and outside his house was a blue MGB. I thought, "I know that car, BCA 566L." Then, I thought, "It can't be." I've got a picture of that car at our wedding, it was outside the chapel. Some of Colin's workmates are standing by the car. When I got to Peter's house he was out the front talking to another man. Peter shouted to me, "Hey, Enid, you know that car, don't you?" I said, "It's Maldwyn's car." That was the first time I met the car's current owner, Dave Jones. What a coincidence!

I only knew Maldwyn for six years, but I'll never forget him. The Welsh dragon on his helmet. He was very patriotic and proud of his roots. The fun we used to have in his company. Colin was an only child, like Maldwyn. I always thought they were kindred spirits.

Maldwyn with Colin Toft, as young boys. **(Enid Toft)**

British Grand Prix, Brands Hatch, 1974. Shadow DN3. **(Grand Prix Photo/Peter Nygaard)**

Race of Champions, Brands Hatch, 1975. **(Jim Oakman)**

With the spoils of victory.

(Dave Jones Collection)

International Trophy, Silverstone, 1975. Through the 'old' Woodcote. No wonder it's blurred. That's 150mph-plus and Tom has armfuls of opposite lock on. What can you say! **(Eric Lemuet Collection)**

(John Dunn)

Ideal conditions for Tom to display his otherworldly car control. **(Jutta Fausel)**

Leading the late Carlos Pace into the Ascari bends in the Italian Grand Prix, Monza, 1975.
(Jutta Fausel)

United States Grand Prix, 1975, Watkins Glen. **(Eric Lemuet Collection)**

Race of Champions, Brands Hatch, 1976. No repeat of the previous year's victory.
(Pete Austin)

Storming into Silverstone's Stowe Corner at the British Grand Prix, 1975. **(Peter McFadyen)**

British Grand Prix, Brands Hatch, 1976. Tom's last outing at his second home. **(Ian Wagstaff)**

The autumnal light always seems to give photos from the 'Glen' a special look. **(Jutta Fausel)**

Dutch Grand Prix, Zandvoort, 1976. First outing for the new Shadow DN8, which looks splendid in its new livery. **(Rob Petersen)**

Italian Grand Prix, Monza, 1976. **(Eric Lemuet Collection)**

ANDREW MARRIOTT

TV Commentator and Journalist

The story I want to tell concerns the terrible day when Tom Pryce died. I was there, doing the TV commentary. I would have been there anyway, but on the Tuesday of the race week, I was approached by a guy called Kim Shipley who was the head of sport for South African Television. He told me that Jackie Stewart was meant to be doing the commentary but his mother had died. Let's remember, back in those days there were no pit reporters. The F1 TV commentary was one bloke. Anyway, they knew I did TV commentary so they asked me. I said yes of course.

South African TV was very new. It was the last so-called 'modern' country to get television, so they hadn't had it very long and had never televised a motor race. They had it in their head that the commentators – and there were about five or six of us taking the feed – should be able to see the whole of the circuit. They decided to build a huge great scaffolding tower which was about five or six storeys high. I mean, it was vast. At the top was a platform where the commentary boxes were. You had to go up an open ladder. You certainly didn't want to go up and down there too many times.

Come the race I'm commentating away and suddenly there's Renzo Zorzi's car on the far side, opposite the pits, smouldering. I couldn't really see what was happening, but obviously, we subsequently found out a young marshal with a fire extinguisher ran across the track. Tom could not avoid him, and I believe the extinguisher hit Tom on the head. None of this was very clear, and I have to tell you I've never seen it since. We did see Tom's car in the final crash, at the end of the straight. There was no word of what had happened, but obviously there had been a bad accident. In those days we were sort of used to it, the odd fatality. Nevertheless, we had no idea of quite what had happened and the race carried on.

On this platform where they'd built these commentary boxes, there was a space in front of them. Suddenly, a teenager appeared in front of me, but he was outside the box. He had a piece of white paper in his hand, an A4 sheet which was folded. I was looking at the monitor, but glanced up and saw this bloke. He opened the piece of paper and on it were three words, "Price [which was

Kyalami 1977: a race commentary that will live long in Andrew's memory.
(Kyalami Press photo)

spelt wrong] is dead." And I had to carry on commentating. It was the hardest thing I've ever had to do in my broadcasting career. I knew Tom extremely well, and I certainly had a meal with Nella and himself that week, maybe on the Thursday or something. You know, we'd come up through Formula Ford and F3. It was a traumatic moment. Professionally, I'm proud to say that I did manage to carry on commentating. I had a producer in my ear. I can't remember

anything of what they were telling me. Anyway, we carried on with a heavy heart until the finish and that was the end of it. It's difficult to know how to put this, but there was one humorous moment to all of this. I don't know if there ever could be a humorous moment in tragedy, but it's something I remember. When it was all over we then had to come down from this scaffolding tower on these open ladders, and a rather overweight Argentine commentator was petrified with fear. In the end, the only way they could get him down was with a block and tackle which was there, so they tied a rope around him and lowered him down. I stood at the bottom of the tower, mixed with thoughts. The guy was brought to terra firma by lowering him on this rope. As he came down, he was spinning through 360 degrees. It was an absolutely terrible day. Of course, it's an accident that should never have happened. Bad training for the marshals, just pure circumstance.

A happier memory goes back to F3 when I was running Colin Vandervell, son of Tony Vandervell of Vanwall fame. Colin was always, to use a modern word, a bit 'edgy', and there was quite a lot going on in F3 in those days. There was a particular international race at Brands Hatch. It was won by Tom in a Royale, which was basically a Formula Ford car with an F3 engine and wider wheels/tyres. It was a surprise because Royale didn't tend to win those sorts of races. Tom drove superbly to win and afterwards Colin, who I think finished sixth, came out and jumped up and down in front of me saying, "Andy, Andy, we have to protest the first five cars. They are all underweight. I know they are all underweight!" Off we went to the weighbridge. I'd put in the protest against all five, including Tom who'd won the race. They were all weighed on the weighbridge and Tom's car was

The day Tom made everyone sit up and take notice of him with a dominant victory in the Formula Three race supporting the non-championship Race of Champions, held at Brands Hatch on March 19th, 1972. In a race remembered very clearly by Andrew Marriott, Tom leads James Hunt, Colin Vandervell and Ian Ashley. **(Pete Austin)**

well underweight, as were the other four. Were we the winners? Well, no. The authorities decided it would be too embarrassing, so they decided to find the weighbridge certificate and it was out-of-date.

So it didn't count and Tom got the victory, which I'm pleased about in the end. We subsequently had a bit of a laugh about it.

I remember, ringing him up once, and the phone was answered by his mother in Welsh. She shouted out, "Maldwyn, it's for you." He was a fabulous guy, very understated. In Tom Pryce, we lost the greatest talent Welsh motor racing's ever had, and a potential world champion.

CLAIRE JONES

Childhood Friend

We moved to Nantglyn, where my Dad was the milkman. He delivered to Mald's parents' house and, you know, that's how you got to know people. With his father being the local policeman part of his job would be to visit the local farms. He would visit our farm to check licences etc...

I got to know Mald at the youth club where we would listen to records and do a bit of rock 'n' roll dancing. I'm sure he would move his arms and legs about, like most boys did. We did a lot of things. Days out to Betws-y-Coed and Llandudno, but we always ended up in Rhyl so that the dads, after they had finished work, could meet us all there. It would then turn into a big family gathering. Every Christmas we'd go the pantomime in Chester. Mald would be on all of these trips.

He would practice with his friends who were in a band. He played the guitar and sang a bit. He got fed up with the guitar when he got interested in motor racing. He was a good singer, but he didn't advertise it. In the summer the boys would practice at our farm or in the garden of the police house. You would hear them and think, the boys are at it again.

He had his little romances in the village and at the youth club. I remember one girl telling me that she had her first kiss from Mald. All very innocent. Later on, when he was training to be a tractor mechanic at North Wales Engineers, my husband, Gwilyn, was the storeman there. I used to ask Mald to take letters from me to give to him.

I lost touch with him when he started Formula One. I wasn't really interested in motor racing, but I tried to follow his career with him being a lad from the village. I found out about his death on the TV news.

I've never been, but people have told me that in the nursing home his mum owned there was a big montage of pictures of Mald on one of the walls. His Mum and Dad were very proud of him. I remember him as one of the lads, always laughing. Nothing seemed to bother him. He was a lovely boy.

The picture of Tom flying at the Nürburgring in 1976 which took pride of place in Gwyn's nursing home. It was presented to Alun Jones on behalf of Tom's parents at the 1977 British Grand Prix. The inscription reads, 'FROM ALL TOM'S FRIENDS AT SHADOW CARS'. **(Alun Jones)**

RAY ALLEN
Racing Driver

Back in the late sixties Tom came to Motor Racing Stables (MRS), the racing drivers school based at Brands Hatch. I was one of the senior instructors and, immediately, it was obvious he was very good, but he couldn't explain it. He was just doing it on instinct. Geoff Clarke, the owner of MRS, put him under my wing for about six months, because Tom had no idea about the mechanical side of things or how to set a car up. So, I tried to teach him all about that sort of thing.

He won the Crusader Championship in 1970 and got a Lola FF1600 which was a twitchy old thing due to its short wheelbase. It was a dreadful thing. I managed to sort it out a little bit. I think he ended up doing a few races with it.

The year after he won the F100 Championship in a Royale, which was a fantastic car. I had won the championship the year before, and Tom took over the car and cleaned up. It was quite easy in that car because it was better than all the rest.

At that time I was the works and development driver for Bob King at Royale and was sorting out the Formula Atlantic prototype. Bob comes up to me one day and says, "I'm developing an F3 car, and I'm going to put Tom in it." And I said, "Why don't you put me in it?" In reply Bob says, "I wouldn't put any friend of mine in an F3 car because it's too bloody dangerous." So, I stayed in the Atlantic car.

Tom eventually got my drive in the Atlantic after, I think, Eifelland Caravans wanted him in the car. I thought, 'Bloody charming. I do all the development and Bob's gone and given Tom the bloody drive. That's the thanks you get!' Initially, he did struggle to sort the thing out. So we went to Snetterton one day, and I got it all sorted and, of course, Tom was immediately quick in it. He was just a natural. Such a natural at it, to be honest with you. By this time, having gained some experience, he was starting to learn about the mechanical side of things, and why he was doing things.

Tom then got picked up by Alan Rees, a fellow Welshman, who was the team manager at the Shadow F1 team. He was extremely lucky to get the support of Alan. If it hadn't been for him, he wouldn't have been in F1. I suppose he might have got there eventually. He did end up doing really

Ray Allen, like Tom, had close links with Royale and Bob King. And he had been one of the first instructors Tom worked with at the MRS racing school at Brands Hatch. **(Andy Ross)**

well in a not very competitive car, but he was making it competitive.

He had started earning some money and had bought an Oast house in Ightham, and had got married. Nella was a village girl, so wasn't used to the glitz and glamour of F1. She didn't like most of the people, apparently. Can't say I blame her, to be honest. I expect it was as much of a shock to Tom being involved with all those high-falutin' F1 people. I would think it was a nightmare for him. He was very shy, painfully shy. You couldn't get two words out of him to make a sentence most of the time. That's just the way he was.

Then, of course, that tragedy had to happen. I was... incandescent. Of course, the safety wasn't like it is now. He's come over the brow of the hill on the main straight, flat-out at 175mph or something, unsighted and, wallop, straight into the guy with the extinguisher and the thing hits him on the head. At least he wouldn't have known anything about it. That's a small consolation. You just couldn't believe it. No rhyme or reason, an absolute tragedy it was. I couldn't believe it, coming so soon after Roger (Williamson) and Tony (Brise). The three of them all future world champions, for sure.

ANDREW HARRIS

Fan

Having emigrated with my family from Wales to South Africa in 1974 you learn to recognise and understand your true national identity. Being Welsh in Wales I had no real concept of this. Sure, we had the odd Englishman in our school, but that was about it. My family was Welsh, my friends were Welsh, and that was all I knew.

On arrival in South Africa as a 12-year-old I soon realised that there were very few Welshmen or women around. There were none in my school, and the few I knew were friends of my parents. In these circumstances you very soon learn to appreciate your heritage.

In 1976 I went to the South African Grand Prix. It was my first motor race, at the Kyalami track just outside of Johannesburg. I instantly developed a passion for the sport, which I still hold to this day. Not knowing anything at all about Grand Prix racing I was very pleasantly surprised to see a Welshman driving a black car called a Shadow, that Welshman being Tom Pryce. He had a great race, finishing well after having to stop for a puncture.

When the time came for the 1977 Grand Prix I had been to every motor race at Kyalami since the '76 one. I had learned all the ways possible to slip into the pits or paddock area without being stopped by the marshals (there were no security guards in those days). I had followed the GP season via newspapers and my weekly subscription to *Autosport*, which typically took six weeks to arrive by boat in South Africa.

The teams used to arrive at Kyalami about two weeks before the Grand Prix for an extended test session prior to the start of the European races. During this time I took the odd day or so off school to visit the track. On arrival I made a beeline to the Shadow pit, where I was very fortunate to meet Tom, talk with him, take photos and get his autograph. The usual things you do when you meet your favourite sportsman. He seemed very relaxed and was looking forward to a good race as his testing was going well. He tended to spend most of his time out of the car, just leaning on the garage wall very quiet and relaxed.

The night before the race I camped at the track along with my father and a few of his Welsh friends. It was very much a party atmosphere. I don't

Tom taking part in the parade of drivers before the 1977 South African Grand Prix, aboard an MGA that was the forerunner of his own MGB. **(Andrew Harris)**

know how much interest the adults had in the race, but I was prepared and excited. The following morning after Formula One practice, armed with my latest issue of *Autosport* – which covered the Argentinian race – I slipped off into the pits just before the driver parade. I managed to get quite a few autographs; James Hunt, Niki Lauda, Emerson Fittipaldi, Mario Andretti, Jody Scheckter and a few others as well, including Carlos Pace, who was sadly to be killed a week later in an air crash.

On walking up to Tom I noticed there wasn't a photo for him to sign, the only space being an unidentified car in the background of a spinning Fittipaldi. Tom and I agreed that this could be him as he couldn't remember Fittipaldi spinning, so he duly signed it.

He was very quiet, but seemed relaxed and smiled without saying anything when, in my best Welsh, I said, "Diolch i chi" (Thanks to you), one of the few Welsh phrases I knew. He was the last driver I met that morning. That autograph must have been one of the last he ever signed. As he was preparing to get into his car for the drivers' parade I ran back to our seats which were at Jukskei corner, a few hundred metres from the pits. We all yelled and waved when Tom came past. One of our group had a Welsh flag, and Tom waved back.

Tom relaxing under an umbrella during a break in testing, which was held the month before the Grand Prix. **(Andrew Harris)**

I had been following Tom through the race and, although he seemed to have had a bad start, he was slowly moving up the field. I immediately realised that Tom was out of the race when he did not come around as expected. From the top of the small stand that I was in you could look up to Crowthorne corner. Crowthorne was the first corner after the long straight, and you could clearly see all the marshal activity, yellow flags etc… I was automatically disappointed that Tom had crashed, but only when the ambulance came slowly around the track did anyone get the feeling that this could be serious.

Slowly the news that Tom had died filtered around the track. To say I was upset was an understatement. Only later that night, on the news, did I learn about the full horror of the way in which Tom had died, along with the young fire marshal. Although drivers died quite often in the seventies it was the first time anybody I met or knew had been killed in an accident. Tom was, and still remains, the only Welsh Grand Prix driver I ever knew.

NEIL TRUNDLE

Mechanic

To be honest, I wasn't that aware of Tom previous to him joining us at Rondel towards the middle of the 1973 season, but he was obviously trying to make his mark and had success in the lower formulae.

He came to us with the help of dear old Chris Meek. Chris had bought one of our Motul-Rondel cars in Atlantic specification to use in the UK. I think it was around this time that Chris was winding down his driving career and was looking to support an up-and-coming youngster. The plan was for Tom to drive the Atlantic car, but when Jody Scheckter decided that F2 didn't fit in with his hectic schedule as a new McLaren F1 driver, Tom took over his car with support from Chris. Tom did race the Atlantic car on a couple of occasions but didn't do that well, mainly due to having to run rubbish old tyres.

He was certainly impressive in F2 and very quickly on the pace. In his second outing at Hockenheim he was the fastest of our five cars in qualifying. The race at Norisring towards the end of the season stands out. For once the dominant Marches all suffered mechanical problems, leaving us with a 1-2-3-5-7 finish. Tom had a great battle with Tim Schenken in both heats, with Tim only getting the better of him when he began to suffer rear brake problems. Tim took overall victory, with Tom runner-up. A very impressive drive considering his lack of F2 experience.

Rondel folded at the end of '73 when we lost our sponsors and Tony Vlassopulos had to withdraw his financial support.

At the time we'd started building an F1 car and Tony, along with Ken Grob, decided to resurrect the car out of the ashes of Rondel and formed Token Racing. The car was roughly halfway built. The tub and bodywork were all done, but we didn't have an engine. Chris Meek came up with a brand-new engine from Cosworth, and Tom got the drive. Our Rondel designer, along with myself and Chris Lewis and some volunteers, worked for six weeks almost non-stop without any sleep to finish the car in time for the *Daily Express* International Trophy race at Silverstone. To be honest, I don't remember much. I was close to a nervous breakdown at that point. I hadn't slept for God knows how long, but what I do remember is that when we came to take the car to Silverstone we didn't have a truck. So, we hired a van and it had a tail-lift suitable only for furniture and stuff. I drilled the tail lift and bolted on some big planks of wood, then rolled the car on backwards so it just fitted in.

I started to try and drive the van to Silverstone for the International Trophy, but only got about five miles and had to pull over because I couldn't stay awake. Tom was in the truck with us, so he said "move over" and he drove it all the way to Silverstone. We arrived late and just about made last practice. In the race reliability issues hit us when the gearchange bracket fell off. It was bolted up but it hadn't been lock-wired or anything, so Tom lost the gearchange. Considering the car wasn't set up or anything, and he'd never driven the car until practice, he drove really well.

Next came the Belgian Grand Prix at Nivelles, our F1 world championship debut. Tom qualified pretty well and was running strongly in the race. Unfortunately, he had a coming together with Jody Scheckter and suffered a puncture which ended his race.

Then came Monaco, which was where the bloody constructors stitched us up. Bernie (Ecclestone), and even Ken Tyrrell and co blocked our entry. Ray Jessop, the car's designer, was busting his balls trying to get an entry, but there was no way. It was heartbreaking. You know, we were trying to get a foot on the ladder, and they were blocking it.

The result of all that was that Tony Vlassopulos, who was involved with Ippokampos Racing, deciding to put Tom in one of his cars for the F3 support race. Ippokampos was an Indonesian oil company, who had a few guests along for the weekend. Tony decided to replace Buzz Buzaglo, the quicker of the two drivers. The other was Hany Wiano, who was Indonesian, so had to stay. Buzz has never forgotten that. He was heartbroken. The mechanics tried to protest, but Tony told them that's what was happening. So I was commandeered into running Tom with Ray Jessop. The other mechanics would not talk to me. Tom had raced F3 at Monaco before (1972), but broke down. When he got out of the car someone ran into him and broke his leg! So, he knew the track a bit but hadn't driven F3 for a while. Ray and I got a hold of this March down in our workshop and the regular mechanics sent me to Coventry. We nearly had a punch-up, they weren't too impressed! Anyway, I didn't give a fuck. We put a massive rear wing on the car, and all these splitters around the nose to generate downforce, which Ray said was all you needed around Monaco. When we turned up with it, there was the March works team with Brian Henton who had a laugh at us. "Hey you buggers, what are you doing? You're never going to win with that fucking car."

We had a very good Pinto engine in the car, built by Holbay. There were two heats and a final. Henton was on pole for one, and Tom put ours on pole for the other with about five minutes to go. He was easily fastest, but decided to do an extra couple of laps and came upon a backmarker who put him in the barriers. It nearly ripped the gearbox off, and tore the radius rod out of the chassis. He went in backwards and the car was heavily damaged. Anyway, I did an all-nighter. I had to take the fuel bag out and weld the chassis where the radius rod had pulled out. It was a good job, if I say so myself. We needed a bell-housing and March had the only spare. With their man Henton on pole for the other heat they were torn between letting us have it or not. Finally, at about 8pm, they sold me the bell-housing and I rebuilt the back end overnight and set it up.

Tom won his heat, but the engine was overheating a bit. He was on pole

Neil Trundle (in blue vest) before the start of the 1974 Monaco Formula Three race which Tom won in such style that the big Formula One teams came calling. **(James Beckett Collection)**

for the final. I think Henton got taken out in his heat. The engine wouldn't start before the race. We didn't have jump batteries back then. I had a spare battery and, if you turned it upside down and put the posts together, it became a jump battery. That was when Nick Jordan, who was looking after the car of Tony Brise, came running over and said, "You can't fucking do that, you're not allowed." I said, "Oh,

fuck off!" and we had a bit of a nose-to-nose. Then it fired up and I was so relieved. I was convinced it was going to break down though. It was blowing out water and I put in some Barsleak. It was magic stuff that. I remember Henton coming up and saying, "That bugger's not going to last." Well it did, and it ran beautifully.

Come the start Tom was off, and they never saw which way he went. I

didn't do any signalling during the race. I was looking over the back of the pits, where you saw them coming through the swimming pool section. He was in a beautiful, oversteering slide all the way around until he turned into Rascasse. That was every lap. He was just... on it, you know. I don't know what he won by, but it was a lot. Nobody won by that margin in F3.

Chris Meek, the late Ray Jessop who designed the Token, and Neil Trundle are pictured in the team's workshop in Hersham, Surrey. Neil and a small band of dedicated helpers worked tirelessly to complete the car in time for its debut at Silverstone. **(James Beckett Collection)**

Rather sadly, straight after the race he was talking to the Shadow guys and that was it. They stole him. We had no contract with him. He was very torn in his loyalty but, of course, he wanted to be in F1. He was such a gentle, lovely guy. Nella was so nice as well. She came to the races. Everyone knew one another in F2.

Straight after Monaco we punted the Token around for a pay-driver. David Purley tried to qualify at Brands, but the rear suspension broke. By then I was completely and utterly knackered because I'd worked my arse off for such a long time, all those all-nighters. I realised I was going to crash and burn, so told Tony I couldn't go on. I wasn't even part of the company, so I quit.

I went to Tyrrell, so I would see Tom at the races and we'd chat. He was always a bit embarrassed after that to talk to me. I followed his career but then, of course, he got some very bad luck and tragically lost his life in a bizarre accident in Kyalami and that was it.

In 1973 in F2 we had a lot of fun. Tom drove an MGB on the road, and didn't have a lot of money. I've no idea how much Chris (Meek) was supporting him or paying him. I would think he'd have been on a percentage of the prize money. Tom always seemed hard up. I met his Dad a couple of times, who was a

Tom, with back to the camera, mucks in to help unload the still-unfinished car on its arrival at Silverstone. Ian Flux is suitably attired in matching overalls, while a tired-looking Neil Trundle models a rather fetching blue cardigan. You would imagine the last thing on Neil's mind after working non-stop for days was his dress sense. **(James Beckett Collection)**

policeman and a lovely man. He was very proud of Tom.

Tom's driving style was similar to Ronnie Peterson and Jochen Rindt. The tyres we had back then were quite robust. You could drive them hard, unlike the F1 tyres now. I have this theory that if you drove them hard and sideways you got the temperature into them and got more and more grip. The tyres would take it, so Tom would drive with oversteer all the time. I remember at the Mantorp Park F2 event he came in and said, "I don't have enough opposite lock. I'm on the steering stops." There was a 90-degree bend in front of the pits and Tom would turn in, put the power on and slide it around on full opposite lock. We'd suggest changing the car and putting a bit more understeer on it, and he'd say, "No, no, that's how I like to drive it." He would just drive around any problems.

Drivers were different then, certainly more approachable. We'd eat together in F2, muck around together, play football together, everything really. Tom was quite fit, but skinny (laughs). He was very humble and very much one of the lads. He was just so talented, and lovely to work with.

Such a sad loss to racing.

JEAN-PIERRE JARIER

Racing Driver

When I think about Tom, I like to remember only good things. When we were team-mates at Shadow we got along well, but he was so serious and 100 percent into his racing, so, in fact, we didn't talk too much. The team manager, Alan Rees, was Welsh, like Tom, and they were very good friends. They would talk to each other in Welsh, which I didn't think was fair, but I didn't mind.

I knew he was fast and he could find a good set-up for his car. He was a young driver with less experience than myself. He put in a very good performance at Brands Hatch to win the Race of Champions. To win there, it proved he was really good because it was a dangerous, difficult circuit. He could have had a fantastic career. I would say, he could have been a world champion in a good team with the right car. The Shadow was not that car. It was fast but unreliable.

Unfortunately, I was in the race at Kyalami. Of course, he didn't deserve to die like that. He was just very unlucky. On that part of the circuit you couldn't see more than 500 metres in front of you because it was on the top of the hill. He would have been flat-out in top gear and wouldn't have time to do anything. It is very difficult at that speed to do anything without losing control of the car. It was crazy. At that time, you had one or two drivers killed every year. It was so incredibly sad

to see young drivers with talent who couldn't stay alive due to some crazy, stupid things. I talked to Jacques Laffite about the accident and he told me that he thought Tom had made a mistake when he hit the back of his car. He jumped out of his car and went towards Tom's car, but he could tell he was dead.

We were fond of motor racing and didn't think of the safety when we were in the car. We knew it was dangerous and that you could get killed, but we still went racing.

The sequence of photos from the Race of Champions in 1975 illustrates what a mess Tom made of the start. His team-mate Jean-Pierre Jarier is almost past him before he's moved – helped by his choice of wet tyres, a decision he would soon regret. Tom quickly regained his lost positions by passing Jarier and the Lotus duo of Ronnie Peterson and Jacky Ickx. He then hunted down Jody Scheckter and was just about to mount a challenge for the lead when the South African's Tyrrell blew its engine, leaving him to claim victory.

(Gary Critcher/Supercharged Collection)

ELWYN VAUGHAN
Childhood Friend

I knew Maldwyn from school, and when we attended the youth club in Nantglyn. We formed a group and called ourselves The Invaders. Maldwyn would join in sometimes with his guitar, which I ended buying (I wish I still had it). He said he would sooner put the money towards his racing school lessons. Colin Toft and the Holland brothers, Brian and Leslie, were all in the group and good friends with Maldwyn. We would go on numerous trips with the youth club, one of which was ten-pin bowling in Chester.

Sometimes we used to practise with the group in Colin Toft's house. On one occasion Colin's mum said, "Elwyn, come and have a look at this." The bathroom had footprints walking up the wall, along the ceiling, and then down the other wall. She asked, "How can somebody walk up there?" Maldwyn admitted later that he'd put his hands inside a pair of muddy shoes and made the footprints. He had a mischievous sense of humour. It's what I remember the most about him.

I much preferred rallying – and competed successfully for many years – to car racing. On his visits back home we would discuss which was the safer of the two. I'd say, "Are you

Elwyn Vaughan (very front, left) and Tom (back right, looking distracted) were both enthusiastic members of the Clwyd Vale Motor Club. In later years, as a famous Grand Prix driver, Tom would be invited back as a guest of honour by the club to present awards.
(Dave Jones Collection)

mad? You're doing 200mph." He would say, "I'm not the mad one. What do you get up to on the stages? It could be a ton (100mph) in some places. You're crackers!"

When he competed on the Tour of Epynt in the Stratos I went along to lend a hand. I carried his spare wheel in the boot of my Austin 1300GT, which was all I could fit in. I ended up not being needed due to his early demise.

When he moved away, I followed his career. The only time I ever saw him race was at the British Grand Prix at Silverstone. I was a farmer then, so couldn't get away that much. I did have some experience of his driving abilities first-hand, when we would have the odd 'race' on the roads between Denbigh and Ruthin. Nothing too serious. I didn't go to his funeral, but I did attend the memorial service in Ruthin. It was packed.

MIKE HILLMAN

Shadow Team Manager and Chief Engineer, Long Beach 1975

I met him for the first time at Paul Ricard when Shadow was doing some pre-season testing. Immediately, he came across as a nice lad. Very contained. Not the centre of attention that many racing drivers like to be.

The next time I saw him was at Long Beach when he came to compete in the inaugural Long Beach Grand Prix for F5000 cars. I think it was Don Nichol's idea for him to do the race. Although, Alan (Rees) was probably at the bottom of it. They thought it would be a good idea to prepare him for the Formula One Grand Prix the following year.

Long Beach was a pretty ghastly place when we first went there. I remember opposite the pit entrance were a couple of Triple X movie houses; trying to keep the mechanics out of them was hard work. The track itself was not very clean. It had holes in it that you could lose a Volkswagen in, which meant the cars bounced around a lot. I'm sure you know, but the race tracks at that time in North America weren't as smooth and as tidy as they were Europe. Long Beach for that first race was really one of the worst I'd ever seen.

In among that background, comes smooth-driving Tom. He had a bit of trouble coping with it. The car was, it wouldn't be wrong to say, badly balanced at the time. It was really an F1 car with an F5000 engine in the back. The engine weighed a lot more than a DFV. It was probably a lot rear-end happy. Most GP drivers had been brought up on oversteering on tight corners and understeering on faster corners. There was a bit of a trick to coping with the bumps and drain covers. Tom did say it jumped around a bit too much for him. We did try and smooth it out and tried to control the back of the car a bit better. He couldn't cope with it the way 'Ollie' (Jackie Oliver) could. 'Ollie', of course, had driven in the US an awful lot of times. So he was kinda used to having his fillings shaken out and seemed to be able to cope with that sort of track much better.

Considering, there was no testing beforehand, just straight in, Tom did very well for his first time in the car and on an unfamiliar track. I got the impression it wasn't the sort of thing he'd put it on his list of what he wanted Santa Claus to bring him for Christmas. He was pretty quick, but the competition wasn't exactly

Tom in action on the streets of Long Beach. A far cry from the glamour of Monte Carlo. **(Eric Lemuet Collection)**

exotic. Once you got past the likes of Mario (Andretti), Brian (Redman), Al (Unser Snr) and Tony Brise, there wasn't much depth. The rest was were you would call journeyman drivers.

In the short time I worked with him it was difficult to get a good feedback on his skills, but they must have been outstanding because of his results in

Formula One. At the time my focus was on North America, so I didn't get to see him race.

He was a fine young chap, easy to work with. You'd be pleased to have him as your son. Very polite and a good sense of humour. Somebody you could give some time too. Then, tragically, he was taken from us.

Tom chasing the third member of The Lost Generation. **(Kevin Guthrie Collection)**

DEWI ROGERS

Family Friend

What is your 9/11 moment? A day that sent a shiver down your spine in a way that you will never forget? Mine was the 5th March, 1977. It was a Saturday and Wales was going to be playing an international rugby match later that afternoon. For me though, the highlight of the day would be the South African Grand Prix at Kyalami. Back then, it was a case of listening to every possible radio news bulletin in the hope that, just maybe, there would be a snippet about the race. Then the phone rang. It was my aunt with the terrible news.

As a motor racing fan since before I could read or write, it was inevitable that I would take an interest in a local boy whose parents knew mine. That interest grew as he successfully progressed from a Formula Ford car that he won in a *Daily Express* competition all the way through the Formula Vee, Atlantic and Three categories – even Formula Two, which was one step down from the pinnacle of Formula One. But never in my wildest dreams did I imagine that I would hear the name Tom Pryce mentioned ahead of Fittipaldi, Lauda,

Regazzoni and Reutemann. It wasn't possible, was it? Someone that I knew personally, reaching the top of one of the most expensive and exclusive sports in the world! That is exactly what happened and I was there to see it myself.

The most memorable period was the summer of 1975 when as a family we followed him to three successive Grands Prix: Silverstone, when he crashed while leading; Germany on the fearsome Nürburgring track where he finished fourth despite being burned painfully from petrol leaking from his fuel tank; and Austria where he was on the podium after another masterful drive in the rain.

The abiding memory of that unforgettable trip though, was being in the paddock in Germany the day before the event started, amongst all the cars and paraphernalia. And who was sitting in the back of the shiny black UOP Shadow transporter in his chequered shirt and flared jeans, casually chatting to his mechanics, but Tom. When he saw us, he came over right away and talked to us in Welsh.

To me, this moment sums him up perfectly. One of the best racing car drivers in the world at the time, and yet, still one of us: shy, friendly

A pensive, serious-looking Tom. Not his usual demeanour. **(Kenneth Olausson)**

and unassuming. This is why he is still an inspiration today, over 40 years after that terrible accident in South Africa. If he could reach the

top of his profession simply through his talent, dedication, sacrifice and determination, without ever forgetting his roots, then so can we.

NEVILLE HAY
Commentator

Tom was a very talented racing driver, there's no question about it. He drove very, very well towards the end of his career. He wasn't someone who had accidents, either. I interviewed Tom a few times. He was a gentle man, a little bit shy. I remember he drove in an F100 race at Silverstone I was commentating on, and he really stood out. There was just an enormous natural talent there, and he didn't throw it at the scenery all the time.

Tom had an immense amount of car control. Just how good he really was you were never going to find out unless he went to a different team. I think everybody thought that Shadow was going to do an awful lot better than it actually did, but for one reason or other it didn't. It was very unlucky, because it lost another driver, Peter Revson – also at Kyalami – who was very competent. He was quick enough to be up there, but I think he lacked the ultimate desire to win at all costs. That wasn't the case with Tom, but he also had more commonsense than a lot of drivers. He was genuinely a very, very nice guy. Not a glittering personality, but a quiet man. I think most people who met Tom were fond of him. He was that sort of person. You can't find anybody who has a bad word about him.

PETE LYONS
Journalist

I did meet and speak with him for a couple of years at F1 races, and he was a delightful guy. Always friendly and open to talk. Big smile, though it was a shy smile. He seemed a happy soul.

In action he was amazing to watch. Just sort of floated and flickered around the circuit, rear wheels hung out seemingly everywhere. Gosh, he made it look natural and effortless.

But I regret to say our interactions never went much beyond, "what happened?" I always had two dozen other people to chase down to pester the same way. So I never sat down with Tom and had a good, meaty talk. Wish I had, should have done, but...

ANDY HALLBERY

Fan

Tom Pryce was in the first Grand Prix I saw live, at Brands Hatch in 1974. He was racing a Shadow DN3 and thanks to my brother, Dave - who being 10 years older than me knew who was good to watch – Tom and Niki Lauda were the two he said I should cheer for. I was seven years old and very easily swayed. Plus, during the Second World War our mum was evacuated to Talgarth with her sister. Because of that history as a child many years later I had numerous Easter or summer holidays in the Brecon Beacons, which gave extra reason to cheer Tom. 'Welsh Mr Sideways' it was for me.

Many years after we lost Tom, when I grew up, I was lucky enough to turn my love and hobby into a career to work in Formula One, become *Autosport* magazine editor and later a book publisher. I don't want to duplicate other stories in these pages, so these are extracts from personal memories I've written about Tom. Parts of this first one was published on the website Sport500.co.uk, a story of the first time I 'met' Tom, aged eight:

Pryce was a very quiet guy, and kept himself to himself. At around the same time, James Hunt came on the scene, who was quite the opposite. He was the tabloid hero, the playboy, the world champion, with cigarette in hand. He was the Manchester United of Formula One, that fans took as their own. But I always had a soft spot for Tom Pryce, thanks to my brother Dave.

In the summer of 1975 my Dad took me to the British Grand Prix at Silverstone, and Pryce took the pole position in one of what I still think is the best-looking cars ever, the Shadow DN5. We had a great view at Becketts corner.

Pryce's pole was his one and only. He ran second in the early stages, and then took the lead, much to the delight of the British fans, including me! Then, two laps later, he crashed out of first place right in front of us. It was a hard hit, but he was pretty much okay, just bashed about.

I went off to the toilet while the race carried on. As I walked I could see Tom sitting on the tail of the ambulance alone, looking crushed and winded. I really wanted his autograph, but felt that probably wasn't the best time. I decided that if he were still there when I made my way back to our viewing point I'd go for it.

He was still there, but it took a lot of courage to go and ask. I finally did it, and he told me to fuck off. In retrospect, I really don't blame him! And it taught me a lesson that has been so valuable in later years as a journalist. Choose your timing when talking to 'hot' racing drivers.

When I was a 'seasoned' professional, 24 years later in 1999, Dario Franchitti was fighting for the ChampCar World Series title. We were at Laguna Seca, Monterey. He was taken out in a harmless accident by his best friend Greg Moore. It happened right in front of me. At the time I was writing Dario's 'blog', and his column for *Autosport* after each race. That crash pretty much ended his championship chances.

He climbed out of the car, kept his helmet on, and started walking back to the pits. His body language said it all. I knew he would have to walk right past me. And I knew he was fuming… I had an immediate flashback to Silverstone as that kid in 1975 approaching Tom… So, I kept my distance! My plan was to call Dario later that evening when he'd calmed down and write his columns that night. It was a good idea – if only Dario hadn't turned his phone off.

I couldn't contact him at all, and I had a deadline and a plane to catch. There was no other option than to make it up, and send it. I figured I'd known him long enough to guess what he might say, and I went with that.

The following morning I got a call from his team's PR officer. They'd read the blog on Dario's website and wondered how I'd got hold of him to write the column, as he left the circuit without even returning to the garage or speaking to the team, and, as I say, his phone was off. Being a bit scared I then emailed what I'd written to Dario to ask if it was what he would have said, and if not I would change it instantly. He said, "Yes, that's absolutely what I would have said." Relief. I know that if I'd spoken to him in the moments after the crash I'd probably have had the same response as I did from Tom in 1975.

Dario has a passion and knowledge for racing like no other driver I know. When I told him my childhood Tom Pryce story, and compared it to that day in 1999 at Laguna, he laughed and knew exactly where I was coming from. He'd just finished reading David Tremayne's wonderful book *The Lost Generation*, about three young British drivers who made it to F1, but were killed before their prime in the mid '70s: Tom Pryce, Roger Williamson and Tony Brise.

A decade later I persuaded Dario, three-time Indy 500 winner and four-time champion, to do a book about his racing heroes. It's fair to say we had a great list, and being completely honest, I added Tom to the selection. He went with it, and captured my own perception of Tom brilliantly. Here is Dario's chapter:

'Tom Pryce: This feels almost like a school essay assignment. "Write about the most unassuming Grand Prix driver you can think of in less than 200 words."

'Tom Pryce is a perfect example of a driver on the verge of the big time, who had earned his colours in Formula One with the Shadow team. Was he destined for greater things? It would seem so, but a freak accident claimed the life of the Welshman in 1977, and we will never know.

'To me – and I've read a lot about him as he is so mysterious – he was one of those gifted from head to toe with talent, like Ronnie Peterson. There are great photos of him on opposite lock in perfect powerslides.

'But while James Hunt, Graham Hill and co were on Parkinson and other light entertainment shows, you can almost imagine Pryce with his slippers on at home, a little like

The British Grands Prix of 1974 and 1975 were both stand-out events in the life of Andy Hallbery. Andy would go on to have a successful career in motorsport journalism, especially in the American Indycar series. **(Maureen Magee/Mike Jiggle)**

Superman, turning into someone completely different when his race suit went on. One of the writers in America shared a house with him at Brands Hatch, and has told me many stories, and it seems my imagination isn't far from reality!'

Personally, I remember that sad March 5th, 1977 day so clearly. My brother Dave – who introduced me to racing and Tom Pryce – that day was his 21st birthday.

(Pete Austin)

DAVID HUGHES

Colleague at North Wales Engineers

When Maldwyn worked at North Wales Engineers I was in another department but would come across him frequently. When he left to go racing I was asked to take his place working on the large diggers and heavy plant machinery.

With me being around 15 years older than Maldwyn we didn't have the same circle of friends, but on all the occasions I came across him he was always very pleasant and a very popular member of the workforce. Nobody had a bad word to say about him.

One of the things he used to do at lunchtime in the canteen would be to eat his dinner, along with several other lads, as quickly as possible. Then they would all jump in a car and go off for a quick drive, usually with Maldwyn driving, around the countryside. When they got back we'd ask where they'd been etc... When they told us how far they'd been we couldn't believe they had done so much mileage in such a short time.

It was a typical factory working environment with lots of humour and pranks etc... Maldwyn would join in, and on one occasion when he was in the stores getting some parts he got a broken brush handle and put it across his shoulders, behind his back, inside his coat. He then put a load of rags up the sleeves to bulk it out. A customer then comes in and, on seeing Maldwyn, asks the storeman, with a look of amazement on his face, "Who's the big bloke?"

Another thing that sticks in my mind is that the tractors had independent brakes. You would apply one brake to turn left, then the other side to turn right. After you had overhauled them you had to balance them up to make sure they would brake in a straight line. Maldwyn would test them down the yard, which was quite long and gave you enough room to get up to full speed. Off he'd go as quickly as possible, apply the brakes on the left side and the tractor would turn around (like a handbrake turn), and he would squeal to a stop. Then another run, this time applying the right-hand brake. Again, same scenario. I was always impressed that Maldwyn knew when to release the brake so it didn't turn over. That was his way of balancing the brakes!

Another impressive thing was his concentration. Whatever he was doing he would always concentrate fully and do a very thorough job. I've always thought that it must have been a great asset to have when he went into racing.

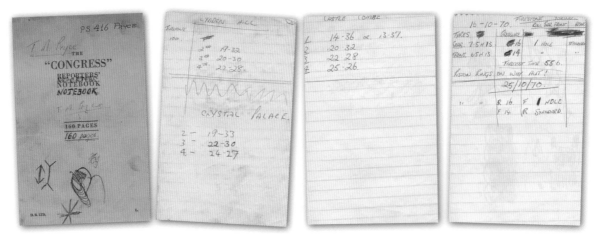

Extracts from one of Maldwyn's notebooks. **(Dave Jones Collection)**

BILL MOFFAT

Fan

I was born in Cardiff and, as a medical student in London, avidly followed the zenith of Tom's career in the mid '70s. Happily, a bus ride to Brands got me to Kent to watch his Race of Champions win, whilst my trusty Hillman Imp Sport even took me over the Severn Bridge and all the way to Epynt to watch his Chequered Flag Stratos adventure.

I contributed to *Motoring News* while still in school, covering the race meetings at Llandow and the hillclimb venues at Pontypool and Penrice.

On a personal note, 5th March 1977 took me from London to my home city of Cardiff in pursuit of my second sporting passion in life - rugby. Alongside my old school-mates I watched Wales beat England 14-9 in the international match at the Arms Park, with Gareth Edwards and JPR going over for the tries. It was whilst we were celebrating the victory in the 'Old Arcade' that the news from South Africa filtered through. I would say that it caused a minor ripple of sorrow rather than an outpouring of grief in Cardiff that night. The celebrations certainly continued. The harsh reality is – and was then – that in South Wales any sportsman who is not a rugby player will be relatively low profile. However, my parents, dreading my boisterous 2am alcohol-fuelled arrival at our family home, were surprised to witness my premature appearance, suddenly sober and broken-hearted.

ROD McCULLY

Bakery Co-Worker

We always called him Maldwyn. I always think Tom Pryce was like a stage name. I first came across Maldwyn when we would catch the same school bus, even though we went to different schools. I was further away than Maldwyn, so we would pick him up opposite the police house in Pensarn, where his father was based. That would have been around 1965 when we were both 15/16 years old.

My abiding memory of Maldwyn is when we were both in our teens and were van lads at Jack Scott's bakery. Our job on a Saturday afternoon, after all the vans had returned to the bakery, was to line them up ready for Monday morning. We'd line them up, Le Mans style, and took great pride in our work. To be trusted with a 3.5-ton Thames Trader van at that age was a great feeling. There were never any mishaps.

BRIAN JONES
Commentator

I first met Tom at Motor Racing Stables (MRS) when we were operational at Brands Hatch, and also at Silverstone when we were running a series of races for school pupils which was titled the Crusader Championship and we'd done a deal with the *Daily Express* to sponsor it. The prize for winning the championship was a brand new Lola Formula Ford 1600 car, so you can imagine it caused quite a lot of excitement.

It was a big thing for him to come from North Wales down to Brands Hatch, it was such a long way in those days. It was very clear to myself, Geoff Clarke (boss of MRS) and the senior instructor, Tony Lanfranchi, that Tom had a lot of talent. He'd come to the school, do his laps and just get quicker and quicker. At that stage, we – Geoff Clarke and myself – put him under contract. More of that later.

Tom had also been coming to Silverstone to compete in the Crusader Championship and was in contention for the prize at the final round which was run the day before the International Trophy non-championship F1 race at the aforementioned venue. Due to the importance of the prize, I decided that we needed some security the night before the race to make sure nothing happened to the cars. It turned out to be a prudent move on my part. We had decided to fit a limiter on the distributors so they wouldn't rev beyond 6000rpm, these were all fitted the night before. The following morning I checked all the cars and one of them had an unlimited distributor. I won't reveal the name of the driver whose car now had an unlimited distributor, but I will say, it wasn't the car of Tom Pryce! They were only six cars in the race, I'm sure Tom didn't start at the front. In the early laps, Chris Smith had built up quite a substantial lead, but then it started to rain and Tom began to close on him, passed him and went on to win the race and claim the prize.

The car Tom won was one of Mr Lola, Eric Broadley's, short-wheelbase cars and was a pig to drive. On reflection, it probably taught Tom a fair amount and honed his talent in a way that we had no right to expect. Getting it to work and being quick in it was an absolute nightmare, but he achieved some good results.

Winning that car was pivotal for him. I doubt whether he would have progressed at all, otherwise. He would have found it very, very difficult to get enough money to buy a car. Having the car is half the battle. I don't know, maybe winning that car and the championship was more important than we realised. It would have impressed people that he approached and it would have helped him get sponsorship, which he did get. And he attracted the support of Tom Smith to compete in F100, then Bob King of Royale offered him drives in F3 and FAtlantic.

Back to the matter of the contract. It was after winning the Lola that Tom came down with his Dad, Jack, who was a nice chap, to Brands Hatch to have a meeting with Geoff Clarke and myself, at which he expressed his dislike of the fact we'd got him under contract and after a fairly lengthy meeting, at which it went backwards and forwards, Geoff said, "It's no good having a guy under contract if he doesn't want to do it because you will never get anywhere." So Geoff tore it up. Even after all of that, we parted on good terms. Of course, we didn't know then what would happen. Our job was to find talent and encourage it. I suppose in some way, the contract thing with Tom, we lost our enthusiasm, not our enthusiasm for him as an individual, but our motivation was taken away. We wanted him to go on and do other things and Tom tended to do his own thing.

When Tom moved down to Kent he lodged across the road from the circuit entrance with Red Webb. She provided accommodation for many drivers over the years, a real who's who. She was an incredible character with a fiery personality. All the drivers who stayed there will tell you they were well looked after. She had a heart of gold but a tongue like a viper. Her husband, George, was meek and mild. He had to be!

I took some satisfaction in seeing him win the Race of Champions but I'm not sure we (MRS) would have boasted about it. I would have handled the presentation having commentated on the race. He wasn't one for drinking in the clubhouse afterwards to celebrate. I must have socialised with him at some point, but in those days I socialised with everybody and anybody. Tom, in the early days, wasn't a very sociable person. He was popular and was liked but he wasn't very communicative. He did speak English, but coming from North Wales they are reluctant

English speakers. Only using the language when it suits.

Some people would argue that he stayed at Shadow too long; if he'd been prepared to move on then other teams would have snapped him up because he had that sort of talent. I put it down to the fact that Tom was a very honest person and very loyal to Shadow. I certainly think he could have been world champion, but I'm not sure he could have done it in a Shadow. He would have needed a Lotus or Tyrrell to achieve his ambition.

I remember the day I heard about the events at Kyalami very well. It was a Saturday and I was in the old clubhouse at Brands Hatch. The first part was an old-style cafe, which you went through to get to the bar, which was separated by some swing doors. Behind the doors were some sofas, one of which I was sitting on. The

(Pete Austin)

Book-ending his frequent appearances at Brands Hatch – a place close to the heart of Tom and Brian Jones – are these two images. The first, an early FF1600 appearance. The second, the last time he would grace the venue, the British Grand Prix in 1976. A dogged drive to fourth place was his reward. (Maureen Magee/Mike Jiggle)

track manager at the time, George Officer, came through the doors, saw me there and said, "Terrible news from Kyalami. Tom's been killed." I couldn't believe it. I just could not believe it.

The next thing was the funeral, which took place in Otford Church. The whole of Formula One, including Bernie Ecclestone, was there, the family, of course, and a Welsh Minister. The Otford Parish vicar was a pleasant-speaking, Church of England Vicar, nothing very extraordinary about him, but the Welsh Minister! He was a firebrand and he stood up in the pulpit and spoke in Welsh and he gave everybody hell. He really did. Hellfire and damnation would rain down upon us. But having said that, it was a solemn occasion. A very, very sad day.

I visit his grave when Karl Jones rings me up and says he's going to leave flowers and do some tidying up. Several people do the same. Around

six of us assembled at the church to mark the 40th anniversary of Tom's passing.

I was invited to commentate at Kyalami a couple of years running on an International Touring Car race in the Nineties. The circuit's changed a bit since the Seventies, but I did go out on to the circuit to where Tom died to pay my respects. It just should never have happened.

When I knew Tom best he was a young man, ambitious and wanted to get on. He wanted to do the right things. It's very easy to get it wrong in motorsport. I hold him in very esteem. He conducted himself well. He was a nice, quiet chap. He wasn't bombastic or anything like that. A very proud Welshman. Such a great loss.

CLEDWYN ASHFORD

Friend

Our two fathers were policemen. We lived a few miles apart. He was in Nantglyn, and I was in a place called Llansallan. My father had to engage with the family when they lost their other son, David John, and that's what made Jack join the force. We were brought up in different places, but used to meet and go to each other's houses and so on. That's how the relationship was really. The fathers were very, very close indeed.

We always went to different schools, and, being children of policemen, you moved around a lot. When I was ten years old I moved from the village of Llansallan to Rhos on Sea, which is on the coast. Jack Pryce was taking the mick out of my Dad, going from a Welsh village to somewhere like that, and within six months he was moved to a place called Towyn, also on the coast! There was a lot of mickey taking, a lot of good camaraderie. They were good days.

When I was in college Maldwyn was starting to race. I went to see him with my father and Jack at Oulton Park when he was racing Formula Ford. From then on I followed his career with great interest, and went

to see him race all the time. When Maldwyn won the Monaco F3 race the family made some special Christmas cards, and I got one of them from him.

I was there at the Race of Champions when he won. When Maldwyn was racing you kept away from him, because he was a very quiet, private person. On that particular day I found a pit pass on the ground. During the race I appeared in the pits, and Jack said, "What the hell are you doing here?" I said, "Oh, I found this!" I was at college then and I had just enough money for petrol to get back to Bangor.

Jack was a rear gunner in the war. He was a very, very brave lad, and a hell of a driver himself. I remember one time we came back from Brands Hatch, and a friend of mine called Elwyn Hamilton had a Peugeot 308.

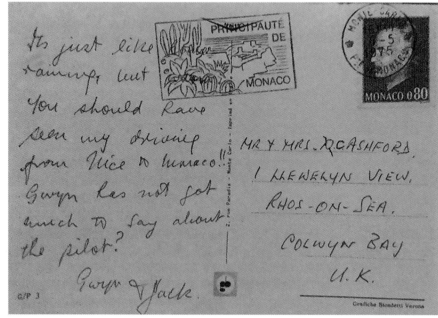

Both sides of the postcard sent to Cledwyn Ashford's Father, Norman. It seems Jack enjoyed the drive more than Gwyn! **(Cledwyn Ashford)**

Jack's car broke down, so he came back with us from Brands. He asked Elwyn, "Do you want me to drive?" and Elwyn said, "God yeah, I don't like driving through London. Well, my god! How my trousers weren't brown by the time we got back I don't know. Jack was a great lad, a really nice man.

Later on in life, when Maldwyn was killed in South Africa, North Wales Police phoned my Dad to go

and tell the family. Unfortunately, by the time my Dad got there they knew. Jack was in his garden and heard it on the radio. Someone flagged down Gwyneth and told her the news. We had a commemorative service in Ruthin. To this day I've never watched the accident.

DAVID WILLIAMS

Work Colleague at North Wales Engineers

I knew Maldwyn from when we worked at North Wales Engineers many years ago. I was working alongside him for about 12 months until I moved to another section. At that time he was coming to the end of his apprenticeship, while I was just starting mine. Maldwyn was four years older than me. He was always very helpful to other apprentices and would pass on his knowledge. He would work on the industrial tractors, the heavy-duty stuff, working on the hydraulics, etc.

Occasionally, we would travel to and from work. He split his time between Ruthin and Old Colwyn. I lived just above Old Colwyn and I can tell you travelling home was quite an experience. He would quite often borrow his father's Morris Oxford. One ride home, especially, stands-out very clearly. We were travelling down the old A55 – it wasn't a dual-carriageway back then – and just outside Abergele, there was a notorious 90-degree bend called Tollgate corner. Behind us was a Triumph Spitfire, I'll always remember, it was more or less, stuck to our backside like glue. Maldwyn says, "Hold on, Dave, I'll lose this fella now." Of course, no seat-belts back then, so I held on to the side of the seat and we went around that corner without touching the brakes and we were motoring, I didn't need to look at the speedo, to tell me that. I remember looking behind to see where the Spitfire was and there was no sign of it. He just put himself into his racing mode. 90-degree corner, around, and he was gone! I'll never forget that.

At that time, I knew he was going to the racing school. If you knew he was going away to the school on a weekend, nobody went anywhere near the clocking out machine on a Friday night, so Maldwyn could be the first one out. You could guarantee, Monday morning, Maldwyn would be the last one to clock in. You always kept the runway clear for Maldwyn!

The worse thing about Maldwyn, and I say this with great fondness, for a guy that could handle a car the way he did, he wasn't that great at other sports. Take football, for instance, in the summer we would pop out into the yard at lunchtime for a kick about. Maldwyn would be there, two left feet! It was in the winter that it became dangerous. It was too wet to play football, so we would play darts in the canteen and you stayed well clear of the dartboard if Maldwyn was playing.

The darts would go in any direction but the way they should.

One time, the BBC came to interview him at work about his racing and he didn't want to know. In the end, the garage foreman got so fed up with it all he told the BBC just to tell him when they were coming and he'd make sure Maldwyn was in the garage and not out on a field job repairing some machinery. That's what happened and Maldwyn never got a sniff of it. We all knew it was arranged. They turned up and wanted him to be driving a tractor from the bottom of the yard, which was about 200 yards long, up towards the camera. The trouble was the first time he was 30 seconds too fast, so he had to go back down and try again. Then, he'd be too slow. He was up and down that yard, by the time he'd got the timing right, he was a nervous wreck. He didn't like that side of things.

I followed his career as much as I could, but I wasn't a racing fan. I took an interest because I'd worked with him. It hit me quite hard when I heard the news because I was going through a bad patch myself. My elder brother had been killed in a car accident in Canada, only a few weeks earlier, so when Maldwyn passed away, things are a little foggy, to be honest. It was really unfortunate that it happened.

I'm sure when you've been looking into his career, you've come across many anecdotes and stories about him and how well-liked he was. If somebody has said they didn't like him, I'd want to know why.

You could never lose your temper with Maldwyn, he always had a big cheeky grin on his face. He had a great, mischievous sense of humour, you never knew what was going to happen next.

We used to have some good fun at work. He was always a happy-go-lucky lad. They were great times, which I remember with great fondness.

JOHN HANKIN
Friend of Nella and Thomas

I first met Nella on a blind date when she was 17, and ended up taking her out two or three times. Then she met Thomas and strewth, that was it, love at first sight. There was never going to be anyone else, and there never was. I stayed friends with Nella and still am after all these years.

Thomas and I got on very well and became friends. He would often ring me up – which is something he didn't do to that many people, apparently – and say, "We're going to the Forge at Otford," or wherever, and would ask if I wanted to come. At that time I was a management trainee in a Rolls-Royce showroom earning £600 a year, so quite often I'd have to say that I couldn't afford it at the moment. Thomas would say, "Don't worry about that." Or he'd say, "Maybe next time then," depending on what was happening.

He was extremely generous to me. I remember going to lunch with Thomas and Nella when they'd been invited out by a motoring correspondent. We all had lunch and the bill arrived, and it just sat there in the middle of the table for ages. We thought the person who'd invited us out would be paying the

John, like many others, was in attendance to see Tom win the Race of Champions in 1975. (Maureen Magee/Mike Jiggle)

bill. Eventually, Thomas just picked it up and said, "To hell with it, I'll pay it." He was like that.

He hated going to the dentist. Eventually, he got fed up of everyone going on about his black front tooth. He had to go and get it drained, so it went white again. Shopping was another thing he hated. Just before they got married I went with Nella to buy their marital bed, a cooker and other household

implements because Thomas just refused to go with her.

The day of their wedding I took Nella to the church in a 1927 Austin Seven Chummy, registration number 1 HOW, and then took them both on to their reception. Thomas had bought a Triumph TR6 in green for Nella as a wedding present, as she had liked mine.

It was in the aforementioned TR6s that we had quite an amusing

incident. Thomas and I went up to Heathrow airport very early one morning – it must have been around 5am – to pick up Nella and her sister, Penny. You come off the M4 and then go back underneath it to pick up a dual-carriageway that goes into Heathrow. As soon as Thomas gets on to the dual-carriageway he does a 360-degree turn. I thought, "If he can do it, so can I," and followed suit. It was then that we heard the police siren behind us. We both pull over and the 'copper' goes and has a word with Thomas first. Then he approaches me and says, "I suppose you're going to tell me you're a Grand Prix racing driver as well?" I said, "Oh no, not me, but he taught me everything I know." Somehow we got away with it, which was amazing really.

We used to drink an Austrian wine called Moselle Special, which came in two-litre green bottles and was cheap. It eventually got banned after it was found to contain anti-freeze. Goodness knows what it did to our insides. Thomas took a drink, but not excessively. Nella's mother still reminds me of the day she found me asleep in the dog's bed. It must have been a bloody good night. Sometimes before they were married, Nella would ring me up and say, "There's a party down the road and Thomas doesn't want to go, do you fancy it?" So I'd go in his place. Nella's mother, Diana, still refers to me as her fifth child, which is slightly strange, now that I'm nearly 70 years old. We were all a bit stupid in our twenties. We behaved badly at times, and got away with all sorts of things which you wouldn't get away with today. It was a different era back then. The authorities seemed more tolerant than these days. We had some fun.

Thomas was an extremely unassuming person who didn't self-promote at all. He just let his driving

do the talking. I had nothing to do with the racing side of things. I did go and see him race a couple of times. The Race of Champions in '75, which he won, stands out. That was a party and a half that evening. The 100 bottles of champagne that he won didn't last long.

My memories of the events in South Africa – which was a horrendous thing to happen to him – are somewhat different from most people's. Before Thomas and Nella went off to South Africa I'd given up smoking. When Nella came back she bought me 200 Benson & Hedges, I'll never forget it. What made her go into the Duty Free shop to buy cigarettes for me, lord knows. I started smoking again then, and I've never stopped since.

When Nella was interviewed for the recent BBC Wales documentary on Thomas she asked me to go down and be with her because she wanted someone with her who was around in that era. She wanted to make sure she got things correct. Disappointingly, she's never seen the programme because she was never sent a copy, which I thought was a bit miserable of them.

Even after all these years Nella still gets dewy-eyed, as I suspect most of Thomas's friends do when he is mentioned, which just shows you how close they were. Nobody was ever going to take his place, or I think ever will.

How most people remember Tom. **(Dave Jones Collection)**

TOBY St GEORGE MATTHEWS

Racing Driver and Team Manager

Tom spinning at Druids Corner at Brands Hatch in one of Toby St George Matthews' Rumsey Investments Royale RP14s. **(Jeff Bloxham)**

The first thing I remember, when I think of Tom, is that he always had a cup of tea before going to the grid and, according to my sister, Helen Bronte, always with heaps of sugar, which was something I wasn't aware of.

I have something in common with one of the contributors, Dave Jones, in that Tom went out with my sister, the aforementioned Helen. This was long before he met Nella. She's now married and living in the States, but upon hearing about the book on Tom she sent me the following memories: "He bit his nails and was shy around women. He was soft-spoken and unassuming but had a focused passion for speed and was ready to give his all to be the very best in motor racing. I once asked him if he felt he was missing out on experiencing life because his only focus was racing. Tom's reply was, 'There'll be time for that after I've made Formula One.'"

My association with Tom came about after I had been racing a Royale RP9 in SuperVee in the south of England, with backing from Rumsey Investments. Mr Rumsey decided that he'd sponsor a team, so I went to see Bob King of Royale and bought two RP14 SuperVee cars. I asked for some works support of a technical nature which we got, as long as we put Tom in one of our cars when he was available from his other commitments.

An early outing in the Royale RP9 SuperVee. (Dave Jones Collection)

I remember very clearly racing against Tom at Hockenheim on the old circuit. The trees on the long straight cast a shadow over the right-hand side of the track. I knew Tom was behind me, but I thought he must have been a long way back because I couldn't see him. Suddenly, just before the right-hander (Ostkurve) at the end of the straight Tom comes out of the shadows right behind me and goes around the outside of me and gets the corner. It was brilliant, absolutely brilliant. I just never saw him. He knew exactly what he was doing. He was a very clever, thinking driver, and a hard racer too. We had many great races both in the UK and on the continent.

Bob King showed up one time when we were racing at the old Nürburgring, all 14.7 miles of it. It took about ten minutes to get around it in a SuperVee! After the race Bob wanted Tom and me to go to Cologne to meet a Dr Schick, who made camshafts. The camshafts were put in an engine built by Heidegger for Tom to use.

Tom was always very clever with his gamesmanship in the paddock. He knew what to say to trip you up if he could, saying things like, "You used to be quick, what's wrong with you today?"

A couple of years later, when Tom was racing for Shadow in Formula One, I saw him in the paddock at Silverstone and offered my congratulations on achieving his goal, and asked him what it was like to drive an F1 car at Silverstone. And he said, "I gave it some round the back and it's really great!"

JAMES BECKETT

Fan

I grew up in Chackmore which is a village between Buckingham and Silverstone. It was only three or four miles to the circuit, even shorter if you went across the fields. We could hear the cars in the school playground. Of course, back then, they were loud, so you could hear them, no problem.

The very first racing car I ever saw was Tom Pryce in a Shadow when Dad took me and my brother Colin up to Silverstone after Colin had finished school. I was only four years old, so had yet to start school. This was a general test day and dad had loaded the pair of us into his Bedford HA van. We entered, as you did back then, past the old Nissen hut and the Silverstone Racing Club office and went up on the bank between the *Daily Express* bridge and the Woodcote chicane. My memory of Silverstone is of the chicane always being there. I never saw the old Woodcote being used. Anyway, we get to the top of the bank and coming bouncing under the bridge – and they did bounce back then – was Tom's Shadow DN5. The DN5 is such an iconic car. The colour, the UOP bars on the side, it's so pretty and purposeful-looking. If I think of 1975, I think of that car and Tom, usually on opposite lock. Unforgettable.

We then made our way behind the Woodcote grandstands and over the bridge over the start/finish straight and into the paddock. The Shadow lorry was there and Tom's BMW was alongside. It wasn't a full-blown 'Batmobile', but it was that type of BMW. We went up to the garage and Tom signed our autograph book. The chief mechanic, Pete Kerr, was so good to us. On his black UOP Shadow team jacket,

One of the stickers so fondly remembered by the Beckett brothers. **(Dave Jones Collection)**

Tom with the late Pete Kerr. It was Pete who did so much for the Beckett family in helping them get to meet their hero. **(Jutta Fausel)**

instead of the usual embroidered patch on the top left – you know the iconic, black cloak one – his had a sticker. He peels it off his jacket and gives it to Colin because they didn't have any stickers with them. Colin did what you did back then, stuck it on the end of his finger and went all the way home like that. He stuck it on his bedroom door and that sticker – along with many others – is still on that door at our Mum's.

Pete Kerr was a lovely man and would chat to Dad – who would chat to anybody – and they ended up getting on really well. So much so, that Pete, or rather his wife, Marcia, would ring up and tell Dad to bring the boys up when they were testing at Silverstone. This would probably be on a Tuesday which was when the Grand Prix circuit was in use for general testing. They did test a lot, with them being based in Northampton. You have to remember these were general test days, so you would have a few Formula Ford cars, a Dolomite Sprint and Tom in the Shadow, all on the track at the same time. Different times!

Tom leading Jean-Pierre Jarier, Mario Andretti, Alan Jones, Gunnar Nilsson and Carlos Pace into Club Corner in the 1976 International Trophy at Silverstone. Just under 12 months later the Beckett brothers would be present at the same meeting when they heard the news from Kyalami. **(Peter McFadyen)**

Tom poses with the young Beckett brothers at Silverstone, Colin to his right, James to his left. **(James Beckett Collection)**

By the angle of the car and Tom's line on exiting Woodcote Corner, this must be the International Trophy at Silverstone in 1975. The last time the classic corner was used for Formula One machinery. By the time of the British Grand Prix in July, the controversial chicane had been installed. **(Eric Lemuet Collection)**

Usually, by the time we got there, it would be late afternoon and they would be finishing up for the day. We would hang around the garage and tyre-kick Shadows. I have a photo of me at four years-old sitting on the front wheel of Tom's car in the pit lane. It had to be a front wheel because the rears were nearly as tall as me. Also, I have photos of me and Colin with Tom. Magical days, really.

From going to the test days, we started going as a family to nearly all the Silverstone meetings. At the International Trophy in '76 we hung out in the Shadow garage. Thinking back, a lot of it, in some ways, is clouded memories, it's like a surreal thing, spending time with Tom and the team. I could tell, even at my young age, that Tom was shy, quiet, but approachable. He was just a very normal person and just got on and did what he had to do.

Then, it all went horribly wrong. We were at Silverstone that weekend and I remember we were standing in the middle of the paddock towards where the old scrutineering bay was and we were talking to, or rather dad was, Trevor van Rooyen and Tiff Needell. We were listening to the Grand Prix on the radio when news came through that Tom had been killed. It was all a bit vague, that he'd been hit by a marshal, etc... Everybody seemed to be thinking, that can't be right, but sadly, it was.

I really think Tom's death changed Colin forever. He was always a really outgoing brother and would be involved in everything and after the 5th March 1977, when he would have been nine years old, his personality changed forever. He became an introverted soul. It really did affect him. Tom was Colin's hero.

The older I got, the more I appreciated more of what he was. I had a desire to write a book about him and had written quite a lot, but when *The Lost Generation* came out, I couldn't offer anymore. I still have the raw manuscript.

It's difficult to chart where he would have gone. The following year, I think, he would have probably gone to Lotus, and if he'd gone there, he would have been in the same shoes that Ronnie (Peterson) had as number two to Mario (Andretti), so that may have made his career or maybe not. He didn't like the limelight and didn't enjoy the fame. He may have had a career that went on or he may have just done his bit and that would have been it. Sadly, we will never know.

CHRIS JACKSON

Shadow Mechanic

I was number two mechanic on Tom's car, working alongside Dave Luckett. My main memories are of the 1975 season, when Tom began to shine. Obviously, the Race of Champions victory was a highlight. I've still got two unopened bottles of Champagne from that day.

We had high hopes for the British Grand Prix that year after the testing beforehand had gone so well. We (Shadow) always seemed to be garaged next to the Ferrari team. After the practice on Thursday, Niki Lauda came over and said to Tom, "Where will you be tomorrow?"

"I don't know about you, but I'll be on pole" replied Tom. And, of course, he was!

Unfortunately, Tom went off in the rain shower. I was on the pit wall with Dave and Jack, Tom's Dad. He was a lovely old boy. His Mum was very nice as well. They were both just lovely, ordinary people.

My Mum was very ill at the time so I was a bit distracted, which led to a mistake with the fuel filler cap at the German Grand Prix. After we had topped up the fuel on the start-line I failed to tighten the filler cap properly and it began to come loose, covering Tom's back in fuel. We had no idea he had a problem, apart from seeing he was doing something with his seatbelts when he came past the pits. It turned out he was slackening them off because his back was burning. He could easily have finished higher than fourth without the problem. He was in so much pain. Typical of Tom, he played it down and didn't blame me.

Before the next Grand Prix in Austria my Mum died. 'Reesie' (Alan Rees) told me not to come to Austria, but I said I'd rather work. I arrived late on Thursday evening and started work Friday morning. I remember Tom and Nella coming up to me and saying they were sorry to hear about my Mum. It was never mentioned again after that. Nella was terrific, and gorgeous. Such a lovely person. In the race we were chalking off his progress. P10, P9, P8, and so on. If the race had lasted a few more laps he'd have won it.

The 1976 season was disappointing. The DN8 was quick out of the box, but we had no money for testing or development. I'm sure Tom would have won in Japan in the rain, but he had to retire when rubber chunks from the tyres blocked the radiators and the engine blew. If we would have had some money we would have sorted that problem out beforehand.

The following season I wanted my own car, so I was number one mechanic on Zorzi's car. He was a waste of time. He couldn't speak a word of English. He didn't know what he was doing. He should never have been out there really.

At Kyalami I didn't cry afterwards. But, boy oh boy! Tom was such a lovely guy. I always thought that he should have had a manager. He needed a 'Bernie' (Bernie Ecclestone), to advise him etc... Tom just wanted to drive racing cars, full stop! Dave Luckett and Tom were very close. Too close, really. I don't think Dave ever got close to anyone else after Tom.

Tom came to the truck once with two watches from Heuer. One for himself and one for Nella. He thought he'd got a blinding deal. All he had to do was to put a patch on his overalls. 'Reesie' went ballistic at him. "Two! Two! You should have got 200!" Tom just looked at him.

In memory of Chris, who sadly passed in October 2020, after a long illness. He would have offered more than the above few words but had to cut short our conversation short due to fatigue and difficulty in breathing. The fact that he made the effort, despite being so ill, speaks volumes for the esteem in which he held Tom. Rest in peace.

Tom and Chris (Dave Jones Collection)

NELLA PRYCE

Nella's favourite photo of her beloved Thomas. **(Mike Flynn)**

Over the years people have asked me how we met. Thomas asked me to dance, a bold move on his part, as not only was he shy, he was a hopeless dancer! Much later on I discovered he was known by his second name, Maldwyn, back in Wales, which the people at Brands Hatch hadn't thought as catchy as Tom. Anyway, he'd introduced himself as Thomas, a lovely name I thought, so he was always Thomas to me, my family and friends.

I'd inwardly groaned when he told me he was in 'the car business.' I'd presumed he meant sales, and cars were absolutely not my thing. So it came as quite a surprise to hear on Thomas's car radio that HE was to be the big attraction in a Formula Atlantic race at Brands Hatch. My initiation into the world of motor racing came a few days later, with the smell of burning rubber and all that noise! I asked him why he'd kept quiet about it, and with trademark modesty he replied that it would have been a very show-offy chat up line; I had to agree with him.

He was absolutely down to earth, modest and self-effacing, which of course was a great part of his charm. He was full of fun and a kind, generous man with integrity and good values; not surprising as his parents were all of those things too, and had brought him up quite strictly. He told me of the time he came home drunk as a teenager, and how sick he'd felt the next morning, but still his mother insisted he get out of bed and go to college. He adored his parents and we visited them in Wales as often as we could. They were always wonderful to me and, much later, when I had a new love in my life, they so generously welcomed and accepted my new fiancé as part of the family, when in retrospect it must have been very hard for them after the death of their beloved son. They were family to me, and we remained very close until the end of their lives.

When we first met on that dancefloor I was a terribly shy 18-year-old, and Thomas was five years older. Looking back on it all now it seems like another life, another world, and so it was really, as so much has happened in those intervening years.

I was soon to be starting teacher training in London, and was living at my family's farmhouse on the North Downs in Kent, not far from Brands

Hatch. We were a large family, with my elder sister and two younger brothers. Thanks to my mother's passion for horses we all learned to ride, even my father, who was a successful businessman working in London. Thomas was lodging at Red Webb's house, opposite the main gates to the racing circuit. Red was, by all accounts, a force to be reckoned with, and not beyond flying off the handle when the mood took her. One evening, Thomas arrived late to collect me, explaining that she had tipped his entire plateful of supper over his head! He was at a complete loss to know why, or what he was supposed to have done to provoke this outburst. As a result he'd gone without his supper, and had to shower and change his clothes before he could meet me. Typically, he just shrugged and accepted it.

When Thomas appeared on the scene my youngest brother, 'Bondy' (Peter), must have been about 14, and the only one in the family to be wild about cars and motor racing. He couldn't believe his luck when a real racing driver dropped into his life, and quite soon became like a brother to him. Thomas was one of nature's gentlemen, as my father was fond of saying, and quickly became part of my family, who all adored him.

Bondy has some great memories of time spent together; setting off very early in the morning along snowy roads, on their way to test the F1 car at Silverstone; Thomas sliding his car sideways around every corner and roundabout he could, in complete control, with a huge grin on his face and loving it, as was Bondy! And once at the circuit, driving the odd few laps here and there, interspersed with long waits in the freezing cold pits… the glamour of Formula 1 racing!

In 1974 Thomas had two tickets for the Race of Champions at Brands Hatch. For some reason I had not wanted to go, and he'd asked Bondy. He remembers the crowds were jam packed solid up towards Druids. They could see nothing but a sea of people, so they climbed high up on a huge advertising hoarding, from where they had a bird's-eye view of Jacky Ickx's Lotus overtaking Niki Lauda's Ferrari around the outside of Paddock Bend in the wet. At one point a policeman pushed his way through the crowd and shouted to them to come down. Thomas apparently made signs to descend, but once the policeman had moved on they stayed put to enjoy the rest of the race from their vantage point. The following year, Thomas won that same Race of Champions at Brands Hatch.

Bondy came with Thomas and me to the British Grand Prix at Silverstone in 1975. Getting in to the lift after dinner to go up to our hotel room, to Bondy's absolute delight, we were joined by none other than Niki Lauda, who was the current World Championship leader in a Ferrari. Niki asked Thomas where he thought he would be placed on the grid the next day, in the final qualifying for the race. Thomas replied, with great confidence, that he would be "on pole position", and Niki replied "Ah, well, we'll see." Sure enough, the next day, in between heavy rainstorms, Thomas set the fastest lap time and was indeed on pole, with Niki Lauda behind him!

In the 1976 British Grand Prix at Brands Hatch, which Bondy also attended, Thomas was up with the front runners but then seemed to drop back in the second half of the race, although he eventually finished fourth. Later, over a cup of tea back at my parent's farmhouse, Bondy asked Thomas what had happened, and he casually confided that he had lost all his gears except for fourth. Not only that, but he had to hold the gearlever in place with his right hand, so he had finished the race driving one-handed!

The Shadow team were lovely, and Thomas had great faith in them all, especially Dave Luckett and the other mechanics, who always worked so hard and had such a huge responsibility for his safety. Many is the time we left them working on into the night whilst we went to eat dinner. Team manager Alan Rees, for his part, had forbidden Tom from skiing, hang-gliding and other dangerous sports, to ensure he didn't have a driver with a broken leg mid-season. As for the dangers of racing, Thomas had always played that down, in an effort to protect me I suppose, telling me that driving on the roads was far more dangerous. Obviously, he wasn't going to spend time worrying about accidents; he was there to win. I had asked him once what he would do if there was an accident during a race, and he told me, without a moment's hesitation, that he would try to overtake, get in front and do his best to win as always. I had also asked him if he was afraid when he spun the car off the track, and he'd replied "No, just bloody angry."

On my first visit to South Africa for the Grand Prix at Kyalami we stayed at the Kyalami Ranch Hotel, along with pretty much all the drivers and teams. There were African dancing shows in the restaurant during dinner, after which I was whirled around the dance floor by close friend and brilliant F1 journalist, Alan Henry, who covered all the Grand Prix races. With his engaging talent for telling a story, and that wonderful sense of humour, he explained who was who in the racing world, plus, who was having an affair with who, as we waltzed past their tables! What fun, having Alan as a friend! But as an innocent, shy 19 or 20-year-old, I was completely agog and couldn't wait to tell Thomas all I'd heard! I think he was rather

This is how Nella remembers Thomas whenever he was about to take to the circuit.
(Unknown)

shocked, and replied, "Well *we* are not going to be like that!"

Although the world of Grand Prix racing was still very new to me I had quickly realised how dangerous it was, but I reassured myself that Thomas was such a brilliant, smooth driver – I often slept on long car journeys, totally confident in his driving ability – that I just couldn't imagine he'd get it wrong. Plus, of course, we were so young and at that stage in life we believed we were invincible; nothing could happen to us. But it didn't stop me teasing him about his poor career choice, and how much better it would have been, given my passion for horses, if he'd been a vet!

I think I went to all the races with him, with the exception of Japan, as a day or two before we were due to leave I'd broken my hand riding a skittish horse. It was really painful, and I knew it would be even worse on a very long flight. Once Thomas had left, of course, I regretted my decision and worried about him more as I wasn't at the race with him, and I felt even worse when he phoned telling me how miserable he was without me.

At that time lots of F1 drivers were taking fitness training seriously, and Thomas probably felt it may up his game if he did some too. So, with great intentions, he bought some weights to work out with, plus a top-notch lightweight racing bike, with all the bells and whistles, but neither

were ever used. He was naturally athletic without any training and, I believe, was extremely fit for what he did simply by doing it. He didn't smoke, rarely drank alcohol, ate pretty healthily, was tall and naturally slim.

Thomas had a terrific sense of humour and could be quite a tease. At times he laid on the 'I don't eat foreign food and only ever drink tea' thing, and of course he did drink gallons of tea, something he had in common with my family. But he was unsophisticated, and that was part of his charm.

My mother still has a small, very faded photograph in her dining room of Thomas and Bondy, with an old moped they used to do jumps at high speed, from one lawn to a lower one. I remember Thomas walking on his hands and doing backflips on the lawn, or leap-frogging over the big five barred gate that separated the garden from the horse fields. He amazed Bondy and me by doing pull-ups in the garage, not with two arms but with one, such was his upper body strength. Between races, back at home, he did not eat, sleep and breathe motor racing. He switched off, and was interested in all that was going on around him. He would enjoy a day at a local Point to Point, or walking the cross-country course at the Badminton Horse Trials with friends and sharing a picnic. He was a keen photographer and would happily spend an afternoon getting some good wildlife shots around where we lived, or of the horses at my parent's home. He was equally happy at home, reading on a wide variety of subjects, and didn't need a crowd around him as he was really quite self-contained.

In 1976 we spent two or three days at the Le Mans circuit in France for the filming of the Hollywood movie Bobby Deerfield. Al Pacino starred as a Grand Prix driver, and Thomas was asked to drive the car on the track. After the first bout of filming we went off to dinner on our own, too shy to mix with the film crew and cast, especially the huge star Al Pacino, who I was totally in awe of! The next morning the equally famous director, Sydney Pollack, told Thomas that he came across so well on film that, if he wanted a career on the big screen, he'd sign him up. Thomas just giggled!

I've been told how different the lives of F1 drivers are today compared with the Seventies, and some people have marvelled at the simplicity of our lifestyle back then. I suppose it's all down to the sort of person you are. Thomas wasn't a nightclubber, big drinker or party-going playboy. He was very much his own man; passionate about driving racing cars, but once a race was over he wanted to get home to our oast

Everyone who spent time in the company of Thomas and Nella just marvelled at how close they were as a couple. They were clearly meant to be together. **(Dave Jones Collection)**

house in rural Kent, to be with family, friends, enjoy his old Labrador, Sian, the countryside, his photography, have supper with friends in a local pub or sometimes in London. He was a thoroughly well-balanced man who enjoyed the simple things in life, and should have been a vet rather than a racing driver!

Austrian GP, 1975. 3rd place.

BP Man of the Meeting 19/3/72.

Formula Ford: Brands Hatch; 01/11/70; 1af
Formula Ford: Brands Hatch 01/11/70; 1st

Formula Ford 1/11/70. 1st place.

Fformiwla Ford: Brands Hatch
Formula Ford: Brands Hatch

TEAC Brands Hatch, 8/11/70. 2nd place.

BP Man of the Meeting

Wedi'i ddyfarnu i'r gyrrwr mewn cyfarfod rasio sydd wedi perfformio yn rhagorol o ran ansawdd ei gar a chryfder y cystadleuwyr eraill. Roedd y wobr yn cynnwys tlws, siaced rali a £10 o dalebau petrol.

Enillodd Tom Pryce y tlws hwn am ei berfformiad mewn ras Fformiwla 3 (yn gyrru Royale RP11) yn Brands Hatch a gynhaliwyd ar 19 Mawrth 1972. Yn ogystal, enillodd y ras gan guro ei cystadleuydd James Hunt i'r 5ed safle.

BP Man of the Meeting

Awarded to the driver at a race meeting who has given an outstanding performance with regard to the quality of his car and the strength of the opposition. The prize consisted of a trophy, a rally jacket and £10 of petrol vouchers.

Tom Pryce was awarded this trophy for his performance in a Formula 3 race (driving a Royale RP11) at Brands Hatch held on 19 March 1972. He also won the race beating his rival James Hunt into 5th place.

Man of the Meeting.

Brands Hatch, Formula Ford. 1st place.

Fformiwla Ford: Brands Hatch 25/10/70; 3ydd
Formula Ford: Brands Hatch; 3rd

BRSCC, Brands Hatch, Ashtray 25/10/70. 3rd place.

Brazilian GP. 3rd place.

Display cabinet at the Denbigh Museum.

F2 Interserie, 1972.

Norisring F2, 1973.

Monaco F3 winner, 1974.

BARC F100 Snetterton, 1971. Winner.

Tarmac F100 Championship Trophy.

Minilite Speedlap, SuperVee, 1971.

Swedish GP, 1975. **All photos: Dave Jones Collection**

THOMAS

From humble beginnings your rise was meteoric.
Your determination was infinite.
You left loved ones behind to chase your dream.
Along the way, you found other loves.

UNTIL...

A love for speed and competition was one.
A love for a special lady was another.
Both were deeply ingrained in your being.
The lady, winning the spoils of your affections.

UNTIL...

In your sport, greatness was just a gearchange away.
In life, greatness had been achieved.
As a human being. A son and a husband.
You were adored by many.

UNTIL...

Unfathomably and cruelly you were taken.
You left a cavernous void, impossible to fill
It was all ahead of you.
Why you? Of all people, why you?

Darren Banks
May, 2020

(Darren Banks Collection)

(Eric Lemuet Collection)